FRAGMENTS
OF
STAFFORD'S   PAST.

FRAGMENTS

OF

STAFFORD'S PAST

by

DUDLEY   WILKS

(Member of the Old Stafford Society).

———

WILDSIDE PRESS

A damn'd cramped piece of penmanship as ever I saw in my life.—*She Stoops to Conquer.*

INTRODUCTION.

IN presenting " Fragments " to the public, the author has strived to put these studies of the past in a form that will appeal to all, not only to the student of archaeology or architecture for instance, but also to the general public who are interested in the thrilling past of their district, and not necessarily interested in a particular branch that a great many histories usually include. The text-book idea has been carefully eliminated and history has been portrayed, not merely as musty, long rigmaroles from old records of documents and files, but shown in all its colours, and in the living memorials of the past and present—links that still abound in the town and countryside. Also, the bearings that one part of this history of old Stafford have on other parts which interweave, and will, the author trusts, bind the attention of the reader from the first page to the last.

The dry statistical note has been avoided, most people not being interested in the arguments authors usually include, as to whether an inscription is meant in one way or twenty others, or that there are so many hundred thousand blocks of stone in, we'll say, Alton Towers!

One day the author hopes to write something of the Common Lands of Stafford, and something about them too, that may astound the burgesses of this ancient borough.

Many thanks are due to John Eymer, Esq., F.S.M.C., for kindly looking over the work and for a number of useful suggestions.

Authorities from which information has been gleaned and copied, include :

" The Romany Rye,"by George Borrow.
" Sheridan," by Walter Sickel.
" Stafford in Olden Times," by J. L. Cherry.
" Bye-Paths of Staffordshire," by Weston Vernon Yonge.
" Monastism in Staffordshire," by Rev. Hibbert.
" Souvenir Book of Shallowford Cottage," by W. G. Watson.
" Historical Records of the Q.O.R.R. Staffs. Yeomanry " by
    Engineer Lieut. Benson Fell Freeman, R.N.
" The Dickens Originals," by Edwin Pugh.
Files of the ' Staffordshire Advertiser," " Sentinel," " News-
    letter," and " Express and Star."

FRAGMENTS.

*" What can the imaginative mind conjure from the perusal of these Contents ?
Motley scenes peep out, of Judges and Rogues,
Battles and Treasure Chests, Monks, Yeoman and Cavaliers."*

CONTENTS.

FRAGMENTS OF STAFFORD'S
PAST.

. . . . . . raining all evening and now a strong wind had sprung up, rustling the leaves of the vine that so aptly gives the name to the old Inn on which it lovingly clings.

I stood outside the front door, filling my nostrils with the exhilarating air, so welcome after the smoke-laden atmosphere of the friendly, queer old boat-shaped 'snug' behind me. The cooling drizzle beat upon my face with refreshing vigour as I bade 'cheerio' to my late companions, whose cheery company, coupled with a jovial tankard or so and an excellent cigar, had decidedly made a more pleasant evening than I had hoped for, staying in a small county town as a total stranger, whose town and people I had never set eyes on before.

Departing footsteps died away in the distance ; the lights behind, which had cast a broad band of glistening light on the wet stone flags where I stood, were switched off, and the brooding buildings around me seemed to be left " to darkness and to me," with only a flickering street lamp here and there, that seemed to be nodding off with the rest of the old borough.

How different, I pondered, was this to the lights and bustle of other towns with their theatre crowds, trams, and dance halls—streets thronged with people—and none thinking of bed. Bed ! How absurd the idea seemed. How early to go to my hotel in yonder high street —" Greengate " didn't they term it ? I would go for a walk and enjoy some country air ; it would tire me ready for my couch.

Thus communing with myself, I pulled my hat firmly over my eyes, turned up a rebellious coat collar, commenced walking up the road, and turned to the left into the high street. On I went, indifferent to direction, alone with the night, silent, except for the chiming of some near-by bells close by an old overhanging house I was passing.

The rain had now ceased, and the old couplet,
> " Rain by seven,
> Fine before eleven "

crossed my mind as the way lay over a bridge and southward, rendered more vague by a slight mist that appeared to be gathering.

A car horn sounded somewhere as I came to a division of roads ; but, being indifferent to signposts, I choose my direction at random and paced on.   A flash of blinding light startled and brought me to a standstill, but it blundered off as suddenly as it came, and with a muttered " Good night, sir," the uncertain form of a police-man melted into the gloom.

The clean air, which had such a salutary effect on my system when I commenced my walk, seemed to be leaving me now, and, as I had walked upwards of two miles, I began to feel rather tired and that I had walked far enough.

Turning to retrace my steps, being just on a large bend in the road, I noticed a comfortable looking seat in the side of the foot-path. Nothing more fortunate could have presented itself at that moment, and, hastily brushing off the raindrops from the ribbed boards, I sank down and proceeded to fill my pipe.   Just the place for a short rest and a smoke, I thought, before returning, so stretching out my legs on the seat I lit up and puffed with relish.   My thoughts gradually wandered from my glowing pipe to the various events of the day, and more particularly to the good fellowship of the evening.   The archeological features of Stafford, and its old coaching days had been the main topics under discussion at the inn, and the queer names of its narrow streets—how the High Street, within a short distance, changed its name from Foregate or Forrad, to Gaolgate, and from Gaolgate to Greengate, and from Greengate to Bridge Street—not one of them long, and a multitude of other curious names about the borough that still persist, such as Tenterbanks, where the dyers once stretched their cloth by the side of the river Sowe that saunters moodily through the town, leaving the name Broad Eye behind at the spot, where, in earlier days, it habitually broke its banks and formed a broad eye of the old Sowe.

Tipping Street, where Sheridan's voters were bribed to vote for him—what a memorial to such a man of genius !   My friends inform me the only other memorials this town has to perpetuate his memory are Sheridan Street and the Sheridan Hotel (perhaps an appropriate one, I chuckled to myself), and also one of the " houses " at the High School.

My thoughts then reverted to the coaching days and from there went off at a tangent to the railways of to-day and the air liners of to-morrow, and how astonished I would be if those two vague lights appearing up the road should be those of the old Royal Mail Coach and not the weak oil lanps of what was possibly an old taxi coming panting along.

Note.—The tanner was not the lowest of English serfs in the Early Norman Reigns, sometimes holding land, English tanners being noted for their dyes to dress the leather with the bark of oak trees. When they make beer-barrels they have to get rid of this stain. Leather was in great demand for straps attached to armour for warhorse trappings, and " wadmel," a leather wadded coat for common soldiers ?   They also dressed sheepskins for the poorer classes.

I laughed aloud—I must be falling off to sleep—my pipe had gone out. Must be starting back to the Swan. I half got up but sat down again suddenly, for there appeared to be sounds of chains rattling in the direction of the rapidly nearing vehicle with the weak lights. Perhaps they've got engine trouble—its the diff' gone. I'll let it pass on before I go, or, better still, the driver may give me a lift back into town. I went into the road and halloed the vehicle and held up my hands, but nearly fell over with astonishment, for the waggon pulling up abreast of me was not the old taxi with the weak oil lamps that I had supposed, but one drawn by four clattering horses, steaming in the lights of two carriage lamps with candles in. Good heavens ! it's an old horse-drawn brake party returning to town, I thought, but now the rumble of wheels had ceased I could faintly make out the outline of an old coach with faded hammer cloth and decorations! It must be part of a travelling circus getting a move on after a performance somewhere. I was about to voice my apologies to the driver, of whom I could see nothing, when down went the wooden window near me, open flew the door, and out sprang the most amazing individual I have ever seen.

I had expected to see a very sleepy, bedraggled circus attendant, but the man before me, recognizing my presence with a very sweeping bow, was nothing of the kind. His dress consisted of what I believe was called a doublet of satin or velvet with loose sleeves, and observed (for he stood in the light of a third lamp) that he wore a collar covered by a falling band of lace. He wore a cloak on one shoulder, and long breeches, terminating in a point, met the tops of heavy wide boots adorned with rather tarnished lace. A broad beaver hat, with a plume of feathers, was in his hand, and flowing hair reached to his shoulders. Dangling spurs and rapier completed his outfit—truly a most amazing sight to meet on the high road on a dark September night !

It was the eyes that thrilled and rather startled me, for they seemed rather to be looking through me ; they were glowing like burning coals.

" Well, mortal, and what would'st thou with me ?" He stood there fixing me with those awful eyes, whilst his jewelled hand fingered a peaked beard.

I found my voice at length and ventured to explain that I had mistaken the equipage for another, and attempted to apologise to this strange individual who addressed me as mortal, for my temerity in interrupting his journey so late at night.

" But, Sir Mortal, did you not need help that you endangered your life by standing in the middle of yon cobbles in the way of my team ?" I then found myself explaining that, being disinclined for sleep, I had walked from the town, and being tired, was seeking a lift back. My newly-made acquaintance immediately overwhelmed me with the offer of a seat by his side, but I was rather reluctant to travel with this strange creature, so I said : " Thank your, Sir, you honour

me with your kindness, but perhaps your way does not lie with mine,''
and then curiosity at last getting the better of good manners, I asked
him who he was and where he was going, for I had felt for some
moments that I was in the presence of a supernatural being, and on the
verge of an important discovery.

'' Sir, you did quite right to ask me,'' he said, tugging at his
upturned moustache. '' I am the ghost of Sir Thomas Whitgreave
of Burton Manor, and every third day of September I return to
earthly form, drive to Moseley Hall, and there wait for King Charles
coming up the Long Walk, so that I may hide him safe from his
enemies.''

We had returned to the seat by the side of the road. I again
filled my pipe, and the ghost produced a churchwarden pipe from
somewhere which he stuffed with my tobacco. We were soon pulling
away together like a pair of chimneys.

'' Pray, continue your story, Sir Ghost.''

'' During the year I live invisibly in the turrets of Burton Manor
yonder, among the dead flies, until this same night every year, when
I return to earthly shape and take from the old oak chest this set of
garments which you see now, which Sir Thomas brought home to wear
and never did in life. Then I spit on the Grey Friars Cross on the
top of the porch, which causes this coach and four to appear near
the Whitgreave tomb-stone. I then jump the moat and away we go
to Moseley.''

'' Are you the only ghost within this radius of the town ?'' I
enquired, becoming so interested in these strange happenings that my
fears were overcome.

' Not so, friend,'' said the ghost, rekindling his pipe with
flint and tinder. '' There is a damsel, fair and comely, who was murdered by soldiers in the holy precincts of St. Thomas' Priory, not far
from here, though many years before I was born, in the fair times
known as the Middle Ages, when the true religion was the soul and
comfort of our land and people. The foul deed was on holy ground,
causing the spirit of this damsel, who could not rest at several seasons
of the year, such as Hallow'een and Candlemas, to haunt the Priory.
The pale form of the troubled body, mounted on a white palfrey,
unseen by mortal eyes, mournfully encircles the ruins of the old
Priory.

'' How very interesting,'' I remarked, my teeth chattering
for it was getting cold.

'' Are you very interested in the spirits of the past ?'' questioned
the ghost, turning those glaring eyes full on me.

'' Very,'' I replied, feeling that anything would be preferable
to sitting on here in the cold, particularly if the spirits yet to be seen
were in a warmer spot than this.

'' Very well then, Sir Stranger, if you will be my guest and
obey without question all I ask, I will show you some more
spirits of the past. To-night augurs well, for within the walls of

Stafford town there will gather at a habitation known as Chetwynd House a host of its ghostly phantoms."

He took my hand in a grip of iron and led me to the driver-less coach with its champing steeds. No wonder that I had hailed the coachman in vain, for this thing was a part of the unseen world to which I was rapidly being led.

" Come then, Sir Mortal, let us away to the merry meeting, away to the ghosts of Chetwynd House."

THE GHOSTS OF CHETWYND HOUSE.

" Shades of Cumberland and Sheridan, I summon thee, appear."
(Old Play).

Away we went with a rattle and a rumble, the ghost pulling up the wooden windows, rendering the interior pitch black ; his eyes alone glowed like carbuncles, and sitting hunched up in the corner, I was glad to think that the ghosts were going to have a merry meeting, and not a rough and tumble.

The scene was apparently to be laid indoors, which promised warmth, and seemed to exclude any church-yard frolics or little games in the vaults of the Parish Church. While I was musing, my friend had made a light and lit a candle in a dark lantern, by which, as its brilliance increased and the lines of the interior of the coach receded, I could see two bundles of clothing on the opposite seat.

" Change," ordered the ghost, adding example to precept by attacking his own raiment. The poor illumination and the sorry jolting of the vehicle, coupled with the strangeness of the garments I had been commanded to don, made the business of dressing well-nigh impossible. However, I found myself attired in a three-cornered hat and wig, which I put on all awry, a black riband round my neck, which the ghost tired in a large bow in front, a suit of what appeared like court dress, the waist coat being embroidered, and shoes with large silver buckles.

The ghost was now similarly attired with one addition. He now wore a much lighter rapier than when we first met, and appeared to be engaged in making a parcel of my clothes and then lowering the window on his side. Suddenly to my great consternation he pitched the bundle out and uttered a harsh command to the horses.

I could now see that we had again reached the old river, but the bridge had vanished, and the horses, with much splashing and noises, were fording it, bringing us bumping and swaying after them. A few yards further took us under an old archway that I had not noticed before. Perhaps it was the bridge which, on this wierd night, had rebelled at carrying folks over, and had left its old position to take up another across the road, making everyone go under it instead of over, whilst it looked much more ruinous and more moss-grown than when I had seen it earlier.

We were again in the main street, but, instead of being deserted, it was alive with men and obstructed by long lines of guns, while the great house where we now stopped was ablaze with light, with armed sentries mounted in front and crowds of gaping boys staring at them.

"Attend now, stranger, on your peril ; we are about to dine with the Duke and his staff ; be silent and follow close."

We then alighted and the lounging soldiery immediately made way ; the unsoaped youth fell back ; the guard challenged us at the door, but, on a whispered word from my friend, the sentries lowered their guns, and, with a ceremonious salute, made way. Our way was then clear right up the stairs into a crowded ante-chamber, so, pushing further through the medley, I found myself thrust unnoticed into a seat among the ghosts, at a long table surrounded by similarly clad persons. A most elaborate feast was spread.

No one had appeared to notice our sudden intrusion and I was able to take a survey of my table companions, who filled all sides of the long board. Nearly all wore a quaint military uniform with sashes, and huge powdered wigs, while one great personage in the place of honour at the head of the board, who rivetted my attention, wore several orders on his rich dress.

This, I guessed, was his Grace the Duke of Cumberland, Commander in Chief of the Royal Army, sent to suppress the Rebellion of 1745, and surrounded by his staff and the local authorities of the County ; who were entertaining him at this point of the campaign in the County Town of Stafford. Servants crowded round, filling the cups as speedily as they were emptied, and I seemed to be bidden on all sides to eat, drink, and make merry.

The conversation was such a buzz, and the inflaming influence of the strange wine in my head made it difficult for me to follow it. Many strange oaths seemed to punctuate the various remarks, and frequent interruptions were caused by the appearance of messages and despatches for the Duke brought by mud-stained couriers, who seemed to have carried out the order on the outside of their despatches to spur and spare not.   The name of the person on my left hand I gradually gathered was Williamson. He was very merry, and I was able to make out from his incoherent utterances that he was Mayor of the town and had been arranging the billetting of the troops in all the houses up the High Street. From him I gathered that the man sitting next the Duke was being bantered by the staff officers seated around. His name, it transpired, was Lord Gower, the Lord Lieutenant of Staffordshire who had been instrumental in raising a large body of militia for the defence of the Realm in the present emergency. Their rawness appeared to be the source of much amusement to the regular officers. A person sitting opposite was another butt for their sallies. This was Sir Richard Wrottesley, a son-in-law of the Lord Lieutenant, and he was also fired with enthusiasm for the Royal cause.

"Your Royal Highness could not have found a more loyal portion of his Majesty's Kingdom to sojourn in for the night," observed Lord George Gower. "Immediately the rebels came over the border, a large and responsible body of the well-affected gentry of the county, at a public meeting, presided over by myself, drew up an address of loyalty to his Majesty, which, when signed by sixty-one Justices, was forwarded to London."

"But addresses do not put down rebellions, my Lord," said Cumberland, "or prove loyalty to the throne. I'll hazard that the district seethes with rebellious rogues that the gallows ache for." He drained his pot and pushed back his chair. "In fact, gentlemen, I have heard this wilderness nicknamed 'The Pretender's Patrimony." This occasioned a loud remonstrance from the Mayor, who averred, on behalf of himself and the townsfolk, their never-failing and constant loyalty to the throne of Great Britain.

Cumberland merely sneered that he ought to have added that it was also the Devil's Patrimony of pot valorous gaubies, and that the fiend had dropped into the Mayor's wine and had gone to his head instead of his 'corporation' ; a sally that drew a general laugh and cleared the atmosphere. No further allusions were made, as the servants were now clearing the board, and cards were produced.

The company now re-arranged themselves for play, and the non-players, including the ghost and myself, crowded round to watch.

Things seemed more and more confusing to me ; the rattle of guineas, and the shouts of the players, seemed to make the oak panel-led room spin round and round. The Duke dropped a card ; I stooped to retrieve it ; it was face up, and I read the *nine of diamonds. The effort was too much for my muddled senses and uncontrollable limbs. Down I went with a crash.

"This gentleman hath had too much wine," said the Duke, grinning down at me with his baleful eyes.

Oh truly he seemed right, a dreadful cold sweat stood out on my forehead, the voices seemed further and further away, all seemed very dark, but I could still hear mutterings in the room. They were probably jeering at me in my recumbent position, the croaking of the ghost sounding above all.

The lights now were out. "I must strive now to pull my scattered wits together. Curse that awful draught." I knew it would finally blow out the candles, the tallow of which had been collecting in pools under the candelabra ever since I had been in the room. I must then have dozed.

RICHARD BRINSLEY SHERIDAN AND HIS FRIENDS.

"Walpole talked of a man and his price,
   Nobody's virtues were overnice."—*The Highwayman.*

I must have slept soundly for some time, for, upon opening my eyes I found the lights restored and that some good soul in this ghost's

*Known as Scotland's curse,

paradise had placed me again in my seat at the table. There seemed
to my sleepy senses some subtle changes about the room that I could
not locate or account for.

The candles seemed bigger ones than the glittering dips that
had previously plunged the room in darkness, and there seemed many
more of them, giving a brighter light. The draught seemed to have
been stopped by a bunch of banknotes thrust in a cracked window
pane. I put this difference down to the heady nature of the wine that
I had consumed in honour of his Grace of Cumberland.

The noise about the room, however, seemed just as great as
ever, although, I reflected, it sounded more polished. Less brutal oaths
punctuated the remarks of those whose persons I was now dimly able
to make out.

A hand patted my shoulder : '' Better now ?'' It was the
ghost. But how changed ! He was apparelled in military costume
now, quite different from that worn by the Duke of Cumberland and
his officers—a plumed hat and scarlet coatee, with a murderous sabre,
now seemed the most prominent features of his equipment.

Round the room were others similarly dressed persons, inter-
spersed by several exquisitely dressed dandies without swords. ''Where
have the Duke and his staff gone ?'' I exclaimed, drinking in these
fresh faces.

The ghost turned ; he had just been exchanging snuff boxes
with his neighbour, who was disclaiming upon the merits of black
rappee, and showing very dirty teeth. '' They are all gone—army,
guns, baggage and all. On the road after the Pretender.'' I gasped.
'' The spirits of all those worthies will be a-riding across Culloden
Moor at this very moment, riding up to the statue of Prince Charlie,
and the Duke and his officers will be shaking their fists at it and
yelling like wolves.''

Curiosity struggled with astonishment. '' And who, pray, are
all these gallant gentlemen ?'' I whispered.

'' After you had fallen off to sleep,'' the ghost explained, '' a
courier all travel-stained arrived with an urgent despatch for the Duke.
He had ridden far and hard, for his horse, which I saw, was covered
with mud and foam. The news was that the Pretender's army was
pushing down between Newcastle and Stone. So instant orders were
at once given that the van guard was to move nine miles along the
road to Newcastle, and the infantry to concentrate on Stone. ' Boot
and Saddle ' was sounded by the trumpeters, from one end of High
Street to the other, and away went the Duke and his staff with the
expedition and despatch of trained soldiery. I went outside and joined
the Company of Staffordshire loyalists, bidding his Grace ' God
Speed,' and away the army went ; the loyalists departing then and
there to their warm beds. It was at that moment that word reached
me that Dick Sheridan was up the street, on his way hither, and I
could faintly see the torches of the advancing linkmen and the sedans
conveying the party. So I ran back into the house again, and found

suitable clothes for you and me, to meet this brilliant company in. Came on up here and slipped yours on as you snored, while these flunkeys were laying the tables for the diners and covering the floor with sawdust. I explained to an arrival that you had come far and were overcome and fast in the arms of Morpheus, so they went on dining while you slept." It seemed to me that these spectres were able to jump from one period to another with the expedition of the inmates of the unseen world.

"So that is Sheridan, then," I said, glancing at the occupant of the chair so lately occupied by the Duke of Cumberland.

"Yes, and next to him his friend Perkins of Rickerscote ; and on either side, Thomas Wright, the Mayor, and William Horton, the leather merchant. Those in uniform, like myself, are Gentlemen of the King's Volunteer Cavalry, only newly-formed to protect life and property in our midst during the troublesome period that the country is now passing through."

I was now feeling much more interest in the proceedings. A flunkey brought churchwardens pipes round at this moment and placed a large jar of tobacco on the table. We all worshipped at the shrine of my Lady Nicotine.

"A most excellent show gentleman, which proves that the theatres of this county are filling a long-felt want" This from one of the cavalry men, stretching his long legs near me.

"Aye, and well supported by the Stafford Troop, I noticed," murmured Perkins.

"How's the new Drury Lane doing, Dick ?" asked another of Sheridan.

"Egad ! Sir, it's not new," said Sheridan. "To-day is its second birthday, and ready for new paint, but there's no funds gentlemen, and little enough for the players."

"Which, Dick, paint or money ?"

"Both," laughed Sheridan.

"It's my first night at a theatre to-night, and I thought it wonderful," said a very young boy near me. "But what curious rules you have. Gold must not be changed at the doors, and it seems to be the rule to send one's servant to hold the seat. Is it the same in London ?"

"Very much, young sir," said Sheridan, "only the crowd is better behaved here, and does not rush the stage and tear down the scenery if they do not like the show. Give me a Stafford audience to a Drury Lane one any time. You see that the presence of so many and so fine a company of gentlemen troopers overawes the rabble, not to mention the enthusiasm to please, that it gives the players, who, seeing such a noble body of warriers ready to shed their blood for ' hearth and home,' play their very utmost."

"Oh, come, Dick, that's too bad," said Perkins, "to plague us like this. Although we county boors have poor wits the flattery is too gross to pass."

" I did but take revenge for the paint," said Sheridan. The bowl of punch which had circulated freely round the board, began to have effect on the company, including myself, and being so engrossed in all that the great member of Parliament said, I was unaware of the times my vessel had been replenished.

" I suppose Harriet Mellor does as well as ever," said Perkins.

" Better," assured Dick. " she'll be a Duchess one day ; and while still on green-room matters, I will let you gentlemen into a secret, as we are all friends here, I hope. " The company rose as one man and solemnly pledging Dick in a toast, assured him of their undying affection and regard. Everyone resumed their seats, bursting with importance and secrecy at the thought that they were about to be taken into the great man's confidence ; one who was the friend of princes and statesmen and a leader of their country.

" Secrets and punch. What boon companions they are," I thought, feeling very muddled.

' Thanks, friends," said Sheridan, nonchalantly. " And now for the secret. Next month there is to be produced at my theatre, in town, the most marvellous discovery of modern times—a play that will move the nation, nay, the whole world, from one end to the other, and render all previous effusions unworthy of the name drama ! The company gasped. Moreover, gentlemen, you may feel more favoured when you know that you are the only inhabitants of this world of ours to share this great secret."

" You speak boldly, Dick, and cover much ground. Is your new pet ancient or modern that it will excel Dryden, Shakespeare, ... "

" There, Perkins, you have it. The play is a Shakespeare—left by that immortal bard to posterity, and only just, the muse be praised, brought to light. It falls to my lot, gentlemen, to have the superb glory of producing it." Sheridan was obviously excited ; he rose to his feet. " Come friends all, I will give you a toast, the title of which will stride all pit-falls, bridge all disasters, and scale the steep ascents to the mountains of fame, and crest on the tapering peak of glory as proud as an eagle on his eyrie. The envy, the admiration, and the glory of our English tongue, a theme for poets, an example for dramatists, and an ever-lasting tribute to our immortal bard of Avon. I give you ' Vortigern and Rowena.' "

The excitement was tremendous as we all mounted our seats and, placing one foot on the table, thundered :

*" Vortigern and Rowena."

And, gentlemen, shouted Perkins, let us couple this immortal title with the name of our esteemed friend, who has so honoured us this night—Richard Brinsley Sheridan." This ebullition was carried with great acclamation, followed by musical honours.

Note.—Harriet Mellor had previously earned 15/- weekly with Stanton's Company at Stafford, with a share of the candle ends.

*A Shakesperian fake, forged by William Ireland.

Seats were again resumed, and the conversation drifted to other topics. The Mayor was extolling the merits of the newly-formed body of Volunteer Cavalry to Sheridan, and how much the sense of security brought by these new regiments of yeomanry all over England had increased, and had helped to render the roads safer at nights beyond the limits of the watch, so that people from afar could patronise the theatres ; it would also foster trade—a subject so dear to the hearts of himself and colleagues on the council.

" My dear Thomas, or, rather I should say, Mr. Mayor or your Worship———"

" No, no," said the delighted Mayor, " I feel that your sentiments coincide with those of my own and my aldermen."

" True, oh King," said Sheridan. " Trade is the backbone and the saviour of our country, and, if at any time any efforts of mine can forward measures to promote good trade and secure extended credit, I assure you all I will do my utmost to promote it." The Mayor's beaming countenance contracted rather at the thought of any promotion of extended credit, but remained discreetly silent. " Trade and its improvement," said Sheridan, " is one of the things about which I sit and dream. Think for a moment, gentlemen, of the merchant princes of good Queen Bess's reign, of the commerce they founded. Look at Gresham and other noble souls who traded our good English wares and made our land great. Or I will take you further back—to the dawn of our history, when the Phoenicians dared the perils of the seas to come and trade for our Cornish tin. We were the envy of the Dutch who tried to out-do us, and now the French try it. There's romance for you, gentlemen ; the business of buying and selling is as old as the story of England, and the name for honest dealing is one of the highest traditions we possess and our strongest bulwark. The presence of the worthy Mayor here to-night makes me particularise in the trade, and future prospects of its development in this noble and high-minded town, whose representative in Parliament I am, and I follow a long line of members for this township since the year 1292, when the first Parliament was called. Gentlemen, I can assure you that if any time during its deliberations should any cause arise, the nature of which I feel would infringe the rights, the liberties of this ancient borough, I would condemn it to the uttermost, and crush its poisonous presence from that Chamber, as I would a viper under my foot. Stafford and its trade shall always be uppermost in my mind, indelible to me in all my strivings. I trust, gentlemen, that these pregnant words which are the pure outpouring of my true feelings will convince you here assembled and all your fellow voters that your great confidence has not been misplaced in your humble servant who addresses you to-night. It would only be right for me, in conclusion, to give you a true Stafford toast that will accompany with it a heart-felt wish of mine, that has been the mainspring of this, my last speech, in this room to-night, a toast that will be handed down to rattle from one age to another.

' May the staple of Stafford be trodden under foot by all the world.' ''

Wildest pandemonium raged ; such a speech deserved an enconium such as I only, belonging to a succeeding age, was in the position to express adequately, and with this bold resolution formed in my breast, I rose to my feet. The ghost, still at my side, however, tried to pull me back.

" Come sir, sit down—sit down." The lights appeared to have gone out again, and the sly ghost was still pulling me—" Come—sit —'' my senses seemed to be falling to pieces, and it seemed, although I could not see, that the ghost was reciting a few lines to the company. The noise had ceased as if the room was empty and only the curious lines that the ghost appeared to be reciting in a quaint toneless key seemed to penetrate my almost oblivious condition. How odd they seemed, the mumbled lines, as they straggled dimly to me as if a great way off.

> " How proud they can press to the funeral array
> Of him whom they shunned in his sickness and sorrow,
> How bailiffs may seize his last blanket to-day,
> Whose pall shall be held up by the nobles of to-morrow."

> " Was this, then, the fate of that high-gifted man, the pride of
> the palace, the bower and the hall——
> The orator, dramatist, minstrel—who ran
> Through each mode of the lyre, and was master of all ?"
>
> *—T. Moore.*

The ghost was tugging at my arm.   " Come—come—come on, sir, you can't stop here all night."

What—what's this bending over me ? Not the ghost with his wig all awry, but a policeman, shaking me violently by the shoulder.

" Wh—wh—where's my friend ?" I stuttered, rubbing my eyes and trying to make out the road along which he had come in his coach and four.

" Friend ! I haven't seen your friend, sir. Safe in bed by this time, I should think.

So it was all a dream then, a tremendous dream, and here I was, on the seat where I had fallen to sleep over my pipe, which lay on the grass. I got up and stamped my frozen feet, muttering my thanks to the officer, who had saved me from freezing to death. I was still trying to collect incoherent thoughts and turned my stiff limbs back towards the town. What a dream I had had, arising out of the conversation about the old town in the inn last night—" the ghosts of old Stafford."

Next morning I realised that I had been in touch with two fragments of the archæology of a town with over a thousand years history, and resolved then and there whenever I came again here, I would puzzle and observe more fragments of such a romantic past that had wrapped around me that night.

June 18th, 1804.
Sheridan's Speech on the Additional Forces Bill.

The people of England know the value of the objects for which they have to contend. They feel from the constitution of the society in which they live that there is nothing of honour, or emolument, or wealth ; it is not within the reach of the man of merit. The landlord, the shopkeeper, the mechanic, must be sensible that he is contending, not merely for what he possesses, but for everything of importance which the country contains, and I would call upon the humblest peasant to put forth his endeavours in the national struggle to defend his son's right to the great Seal of England.

Note 1.—Sheridan during election contests usually occupied two rooms on the first floor of No. 6, Eastgate. From a window in this house he often addressed the burgesses.

Note 2.—He also obtained for his constituents many orders for shoes, especially his friend Horton.

In my library I one day came across some particulars of the Civil Wars, and a chapter of King Charles at Stafford in which I at once became absorbed.

KING CHARLES I. AT STAFFORD.

" To teach my flock I never missed,
Kings are by God appointed,
And lost are those that dare resist
Or touch the Lord's Anointed."
—*Vicar of Bray.*

The fierce quarrel between King Charles the First and his Parliament grew to a head, and the year 1642 shows Charles, having finally split with Parliament, quitting London with his Guards and friends, quite a small force, to unfurl his standard at Nottingham on the 25th August.

His enemies were already a force of fifteen thousand men (the King had 550), stationed at Northampton, and were commanded by a steady but stupid Staffordshire nobleman, Robert Devereux, Earl of Essex, Commander in Chief of the Parliamentary Forces and Lord High Steward of the town of Stafford.

Essex, whose home was at Chartley Castle, situated some seven miles from Stafford, was 50 years old, a soldier of experience and a great hunter.

Son of the Essex of Elizabethan fame, he married at the age of fourteen, Frances, daughter of Thomas Howard, Duke of Suffolk. Children were often married at tender ages in those days.

His married life proving unhappy, Essex returned to the seclusion of Chartley after the divorce, where he resided in great magnificence.

His wife had procured the divorce with the King's aid, and this would probably embitter the Earl against Charles and would partly explain his early appearance in the field when other men were making up their minds on which side to throw their weight. An experienced leader, he had, at the age of twenty-eight, raised two companies of gentlemen adventurers for service in the Palatinate, with his friend the Earl of Oxford, and several times had led his own men in Holland.

At the outbreak of the Civil War, he was appointed to the command of the army by Parliament, and at once took up his command.

Up against this serious menace, and outnumbered by about 20 to 1, Charles retreated from Nottingham to Derby and thence to Uttoxeter, where he stayed one night. His arrival at that ancient market town of so many pronunciations, was marked by a merry peal on the bells of the Parish Church. The town guard went out to meet him, and escorted the Royal Army into the town.

There is a record in the " Uttoxeter Chronicle " of 5s. being paid to the Ringers for this loyal service, and the authorities also provided everything for their comfort ; nothing being spared.

Next morning 34s. 6d. was paid to the county trained bands to guard the King on the fourteen miles of road between that town and Stafford. These men were often persuaded to join the Royal Forces at the end of their duty, sometimes forcibly, and if that extreme measure failed, their arms and equipment would be wrested from them and they would be driven away with blows and curses for their disloyalty.

Charles, with this piece of strategy in view, would always, when crossing the border from one county into another, in his marches, courteously request the trained bands of that county to attend him, and, either during, or at the end of their duty, test their loyalty in this manner.

The King set out for Stafford along the narrow winding and hilly road through Chartley, crossing the Trent again at Weston. This road was barely good enough for even a cart track during the summer, it being the month of August, but in winter was often impassable ; fallen trees lay across it, while great holes and huge ruts harrassed the way of the traveller. Some of the soldiers had to walk alongside the coaches and keep them from overturning by applying their shoulders at rough places.

Chartley, of course, brought them to the residence of their most formidable enemy of the moment, and the troops fully expected they would be allowed to pillage it. They were mistaken, for the King would allow no such outrage.

The Royal Historian records that the Cavaliers were very upset over this, and their glum looks did not pass away until the nearness of Stafford reminded them of further good cheer.

The King was setting an example in good behaviour. Perhaps he and his two nephews, Rupert and Maurice, were too busy recruiting at all the villages and farmsteads they passed to stop pillaging. That would only lose time. It took them a day to reach Stafford from Uttoxeter as it was. At Weston a troop of horse with the Commissioner and his staff were sent on to acquaint the Stafford authorities of the King's approach, to commandeer supplies if necessary, and arrange for the billeting of all the King's horses and all the King's men. As they mounted the rugged way to the top of Weston Bank they jeered and laughed at a grisly corpse coated with pitch, swaying in an iron basket, suspended by chains.

At Stafford a hurried meeting of the Town Council was convened, with the High Bailiffs, Mayor, etc., who decided that " If His Majesty came to the Town, he shall have access to it, and have the best entertainment the troublesome times afford."

They then gave ear to the Commissioner, who requested them to supply, among other things, 10,000 pennyworth of bread. To obtain this large amount the Municipal authorities had to despatch messengers to Lichfield, Penkridge, and Wolverhampton for supplies. The quantity, however, eventually exceeded the amount required and the remainder was disposed of at a loss of 8/6.

Some hours later the Chief Dignitaries of the Town, including the High Bailiffs, on horseback, and the Recorder, attended by the Sergeant of Mace, the Town Crier, and the Town Chamberlain, preceded by a posse of Javelin men, formed an imposing procession. This procession ceremoniously wended its way down Eastgate Street to the East Gate, where they dismounted to await the King's arrival. The old East Gate (parts of which still remain, including the groove for the portcullis) would be smartened up for the occasion, probably by the Town arms being set up on it. The East Gate was built on a solid bank of sand on a pavement of stone extending 3ft. beyond, upon which the 18 inch spikes of the portcullis rested when lowered.

A fanfare of trumpets announced the royal approach, and soon Michael Wolrich, the Mayor, was introducing himself and his brethren to King Charles and the Princes, Rupert and Maurice. Rupert was 23 years of age, and was General of the King's Horse. Prince Rupert's black flag was carried after the Royal Trumpeters.

The Mace in the Royal presence would be first reversed, as was the custom, and then handed up to His Majesty.

There was no Lord High Steward to conduct the ceremonies as on all Royal visits hitherto, and to bear the Sword of State before the King, as that gentleman, at that very moment, was hurrying after the King with an increased army and a sword of a very different temper from the one carried before the King on such occasions. The Mace which was handed up to the King was at that time quite new and very valuable, being richly chased (Note—Mace lost long after) and inscribed, and we can imagine how Charles, who was at that time so short of money, would look at it, making at the same time a mental appraisement of its value. He kissed and returned it to the town authorities. It was then borne before him up Eastgate Street and through the Market Square round to the Ancient High House, where he was to stay.

This was not the first visit to Stafford of the King, for he had stayed here the previous year, probably coming from Tutbury Castle, where he usually resided on his hunting expeditions in Staffordshire.

At the High House he was received and welcomed by one of the members of Parliament for Stafford, Captain Richard Sneyd, a scion of one of the oldest families in the county.

The town house of the Sneyds of Keele was to be the headquarters of the King, his advisers, and Staff for the next three days, and a more beautiful house could not be found in which to entertain Royalty than the Ancient High House, built by Richard Donnington in 1555. The name Sneyd—pronounced Sneed—is Saxon, the word meaning sythe, and this sythe appears emblazoned on a shield still remaining above the doorway of the Greengate entrance to the house.

In the space in the centre of the sythe there is a fleur-de-lis, denoting the service of earlier holders of the name in the old French wars.*

Apart from the King's regular attendances at the Parish Church of St. Mary's hard by, very little is heard concerning him during his stay. Very possibly most of his time was spent closeted with his sole remaining minister writing despatches, threatening or entreating, to both friends and enemies.

Meanwhile, the zeal displayed in recruiting by Prince Rupert and his brother Maurice from the first moment that they had themselves joined with their uncle, was the means of considerably increasing the King's forces.

An order preserved in the William Salt Library at Stafford, from Charles the First to Prince Rupert, is still extant,* dated September 18th A.D. 1642, requiring him to give orders for 8 Troops of Horse and 5 Troops of " Dragooners " to march towards Nantwich from Stafford.

Such orders would be consigned to waiting couriers in Greengate, who would immediately ride off to their destination.

The short distance between the Ancient High House and St. Mary's was strewn with rushes by an old woman, who received one shilling for brightening things up, and the King, attended by Varney, the Knight Marshall, the royal staff, and a numerous guard marched in State to church each morning for service.

The 90th and 91st Psalms were read, and their comforting words, in that solemn fane :

*Note—The fleur-de-lis were first granted at the siege of Acre in 1191. These lilies of France are supposed to be the lovely yellow iris.

*See apendix. " King Charles' letter to Prince Rupert."

> Lord, Thou hast been our refuge,
> Oh, satisfy us with Thy mercy,
> Comfort us again after the time
> That Thou has plagued us

must have poured balm on the King's troubled mind.

At the rear of the High House at that time was a large garden, where the King and others enjoyed the air in their spare moments away from the cares of war and state craft.

One afternoon the King was walking round it with Rupert, when the weather cock on the Spire of St. Mary's tower caught the eye of the latter and, drawing a pistol, he put a hole clean through it, at a distance of some sixty yards, the hole being visible to those in the garden below. The King judged it a fluke, but Rupert proved the contrary by matching it with another, the two holes being plainly seen. It shows the insecurity of the times when a Prince, not engaged in any special duty, carried pistols.

Charles did not visit Stafford Castle during his stay, as, although it was held by known loyalists, the Stafford family, who were Roman Catholics, and he would not wish to prejudice his cause by openly acknowledging them, because of the religious intolerance of the times.

Throughout the Wars he had great assistance from the catholics of this country. Probably he met Lady Stafford, who was commander of the garrison, secretly during his stay, perhaps by the secret underground passage that rumour has it, existed between the Castle, the Church and the High House. Old sewers often came to be romantically called secret passages. She certainly defended it later, and then, with all her people and valuables, disappeared, leaving an evacuated castle to the surrounding ring of Roundhead forces.

Later on, at Shrewsbury, Charles told the people he would not suffer an army of papists to be raised, at the same time communicating with the Earl of Newcastle in the north urging him to enlist without any regard to the religion of the troops, all the men he could get. He dared not himself encourage the enrolling of Catholics, owing to the bitterness of feeling, even by many of his own party, against them ; but during his early reign he had always been lenient to Roman Catholics, which brought them whole-heartedly to his side in his troubles with Parliament.

On Friday, the 18th, the King and his army left Stafford, passing the castle on their way to Wellington, with the Royal Colours floating on the battlements and every eye in its garrison strained in the King's direction. Three days later, at Wellington, the King made a speech to the people after the Orders for the Day had been read.

He told them for their comfort that they should meet no enemies but traitors, most of them Brownists, Anabaptists or Atheists, who would destroy both Church and Commonwealth.

He then made one of his solemn protestations, imprecating the vengeance of Heaven upon himself and his prosterity if his intentions were not solely for the maintenance of the true reformed Protestant religion established in the Church of England, the laws and liberties of the Kingdom, and the just privileges of Parliament.

These open speeches did Charles much good, and the laying of his cards on the table, so to speak, brought many adherents to his cause.

From there the King removed to Shrewsbury, his forces having risen to 8,000, besides horses, etc.

Thus passes King Charles and his clarion call to arms from our pages, leaving the seeds of war and tumult behind him, newly-found friends and fewer enemies, also a great many neutrals, whom the civil war was not yet to disturb. These, in their midland isolation, cared little who ruled them and thought not of the morrow.

Following are extracts from the old records of the Corporation, and the Churchwardens' Records, giving the interesting details of payments made during the King's visit and after.

1641—2. Item, of several inhabitants of the Towne since the King went hence towards charges and money laid out when his Majetie was at Stafford   ...   10   10   8

1642. To Elizabeth Jones for Rushes to Straw in his Maj. way to Church   0   1   0
For a messenger to Lichfield to provide bread   ...   0   2   6
Against his Maj'ties cominge Mr. Leonard Picknay, his Maj'ties Commissary, sent a command into this towne to provide 10,000 pennyworth of breade for the next day, some whereof was spared, by which there was lost in selling of it   0   8   6
Paid John Clerke for goinge to Penkrich and Wolverhampton to speake for bread   0   2   6
Re'd of the Compy and some O'rs of the Towne for the fortifyinge thereof by several Sommes as appeareth by a note   45   10   0
In money to buy drinke and in bread and cheese for the Guardes   0   10   10
Pd for beare bestowed upon Countrymen and O'rs when S'r Francis Wortley was cominge   0   2   8
Given the townsmen and countrymen att the same time about 4lb. and halffe of powder, bullett, and shott   0   8   0
Given unto the Princes' Trumpeters   0   10   0
Pd for beare and spice, bestowed on Capts Lane and Fouke and other Charges   0   1   6
Pd for Coles delivered to the Guard at several times when the King's party was here, which should have been all'd of on Garrison Money   ...   0   7   6

THE BATTLE OF HOPTON HEATH.

" And now we come to Hopton Heath,
Where many poor warriors lie beneath,
On the 19th March, 1643
The men fought hard for liberty.

If the relics of this battle
The visitors would like to see,
Please ask the Landlord,
And he will show it thee."
                              T. Ward, Tinkerborough.

Some weeks later, while the ghastly dream I had had in Stafford was still a poignant memory, I received a manuscript from one of the friends I had made in the Vine, with the above heading, a title of so promising a chapter that I at once sat down and forgot myself in the following matter :—

At a small inn, situated in the midst of a hamlet known as Salt, not far from the town of Stafford, is a card, fastened on the wall in the bar, bearing the above lines.

The relics, to which the lines allude, consist of a woodman's knife, bound by silver wire and with the remains of a whistle in the handle ; there is also a broad-bladed knife like the present-day Ghurka's. These relics were found in the thatch above the rafters some years ago, and the house is very proud of them. They are connected with rather an obscure action that was fought near here on what is partly known as Hopton Heath and partly Salt Heath, during the great Civil Wars between King and Parliament. Its importance and numbers cannot be reckoned with such battles as Edgehill and Marston Moor, but as one of the lesser engagements that drained both sides up and down the country, it was as fierce and bloody as any. Neverthe-less, it is extremely interesting to readers and lovers of Stafford and its beautiful district, but it is astonishing that so little is known of it.

Records of the different survivors vary very much, and in one case even the date in the Church Register gives it a year beforehand—that of Sandon Church.

The fight was in March, 1643, but the Register says March, 1642, a month you notice before the Civil Wars commenced.

It is necessary, however, to give some of the events that led up to this blood-thirsty action, for Stafford saw the ominous signs of bloody work at the very commencement of the year 1643.

The county families in Staffordshire were mixed in their political feelings towards the great questions of the day. About 40 Lords and other great ones were ranged on the side of Parliament, and 28 unfurled the King's colours. Tutbury Castle was held by Lord Loughborough; Stafford Castle, as we have already stated, by Lady Stafford ; and Dudley Castle by Colonel Leveson, who was supposed also to hold Stafford, Wolverhampton and Lilleshall Abbey.

The Close of Lichfield Cathedral was garrisoned by Lord Chesterfield ; Leek was a stronghold of Roundheads, while Burton, throughout the war, remained a bone of contention to both sides. Burton was of great stratgetic importance, being constantly taken and retaken, and subject to many sudden assults.

The remainder of 1642 had passed away quietly as far as Stafford is concerned, for Charles had made an abortive attempt on London after Edgehill, and had retired to Oxford, which he made his capital, a very good alternative at that time one can imagine, for Oxford always was a stately city.

The only happening of moment in Stafford was an order from the gallant Lord Falkland to " ease " the town of post-horses and carriages, the charge for proclaiming the warrant in the Market Square being 3s. 6d.

Old records by a Town Chamberlain show a degrading quarrel between local magistrates, one accusing the other of proclaiming King Charles a traitor in the Market Square. Perhaps the murmuring over the town's expenses through the Royal visit and the carrying out of Lord Falkland's warrant, produced this high feeling. The post-chaise business must have been a rapidly rising one in Stafford even at this date to have occasioned the Warrant.

The passing of winter began to stimulate all partizans, and the G.H.Q. at Oxford received letters from all sources asking for assistance in fortifying homes and strongholds.

January, 1643, saw a hopeless attempt to formulate a treaty at Oxford, while royalists melted down their plate in the royal cause, and the Queen's jewels were pawned at Antwerp.

In reply to an entreating letter from the royalists besieged in Lichfield Close, the Earl of Northampton (who commanded a strong force of horse totalling about 900 raised and equipped by himself, many being retainers and tenants, accustomed to the saddle and used to bearing arms) was ordered to proceed to their relief. The relieving expedition was, however, sent too late to succour the defenders of the Close. Northampton reached Coleshill in Staffordshire ten days after the weak Earl of Chesterfield, who commanded, had surrendered to the rebels, after a three days siege ; the besieged being allowed to march out with all honours.

Chesterfield retreated to Stafford, whence he was followed by Sir John Gell, bent on following up the advantage gained by the Roundheads. The Earl of Northampton, learning this, came on to Stafford in time to fall suddenly on Gell's force, causing it to retire with a loss of 100 men. Gell hurriedly fell back towards Cheshire, where he joined a force under a Deputy Lieutenant of Cheshire, Sir William Brereton, making between them 3,000 strong.

Sir William Brereton, a member of Parliament for that county, had also been successful in beating Sir Thomas Aston in January, a Royalist in command of the King's Dragoons, and had the added impetus of success. Sir John Gell was also a member of Parliament for Derby and had raised a force for Parliament.

Gell's men are described in Hutchinson's Memoirs as good stout fighting men, but the most ungovernable wretches that belonged to the Parliament. '' He himself, nor no man, knows for what reason he chose that side, for he had not understanding enough to judge the equity of the cause, no piety or holiness, being a foul adulterer all the time he served the Parliament, and so unjust that, without any remorse, he suffered his men to plunder both honest men and cavaliers.'' He and his men were the type to whom Cromwell alluded when he said that the army was full of '' tavern servants and beer swillers.''

To this formidable and overwhelming force the Earl of Northampton found himself in close proximity.

It would be interesting to find why Northampton came on to Stafford, apart from linking up with the remnants from Lichfield Close, because he could not have defended Stafford, even when he had it, with a body of cavalry. Whilst in Stafford, however, the Earl learnt, by sending out reconnaissance parties, that 200 Roundheads had gathered at Haywood, a force upon which he fell suddenly on Friday, the 17th of March, at some unknown point, slaying half their number, the rest escaping by difficult byways in which that district abounds.

So, with two minor victories to his credit, the Earl would feel that he was accomplishing good work, and, returning to Stafford, rested his troops.

Sunday dawned calm and peaceful, with the weather rather frosty. The inhabitants, as usual, made their several ways to the Churches of St. Mary's and St. Chad's. Daniel Bailey was the Rector of the former and was soon to be dispossessed of his lovely Church and living.

The Earl's troops remained under arms and ready to move off at a moment's notice, the Earl not being too sure of his position. Suddenly, at 12 o'clock, intelligence was received that Sir John Gell was marching through Sandon, defiling the monuments in the church as he passed, and proceeding up Hopton Bank. They had already refreshed themselves at the old Dog and Doublet Inn at Sandon, where, not content with draining quart pots, they had plunged their heads into the great vats in the cellar and drank the ale.

The scouts had only spotted Sir John's force, and after watching them swilling at the inn, and seen their further direction, had ridden madly back to Stafford to inform the Earl. Northampton, under the impression that Gell had recruited his forces with Moorlanders, and was simply round the county on a pillaging foray, as was his wont, and learning also of their debaucheries at Sandon, saw that they would be an easy pray for his cavalry.

'' Boot and Saddle '' was sounded in the Market Square, and the townsfolk, as they came out of church, saw the Earl's troops cantering down the High Street to the East Gate, through which they galloped and spurred along the Weston Road.

The rear was commanded by Sir Thomas Byron, who clattered along after them with the light baggage and the spare horses.

In any case, the Earl could not have remained in the town. To use his force effectively, he must withdraw or advance into the open, where his forces were most formidable. In advancing, he had reckoned without Sir William Brereton and his artillery and infantry, about whom he had apparently heard nothing.

Three miles along the Weston Road the Earl turned left on to an open heath, known on old maps as St. Amon's Heath (no one knows why) but generally as Hopton Heath. Immediately the Earl's staff reconnoitred the position, and found, to their dismay, not only Gell's force, but also the force of Sir William Brereton drawn up facing them in a square. This formation was composed of artillery, backed by a formidable army of pikemen, while radiating from them were hedges that completely hid the musketeers on the right wing. A low wall on the left, with Gell's cavalry behind, formed the reserve —truly a formidable array.

A hurried council of war was held by the royalists, and it was decided to send out feelers. Small parties of skirmishers were ordered to scour the hedges on the right and the wall on the left to draw the fire. No sooner had the skirmishers neared the innocent hedges than spurts of flame swept the patrols and riderless horses came careering back.

This manœuvre told the royalists all they wished to know, and an order was made for the whole force, with the exception of Sir John Byron's Reserve, to advance in two parts, one against the wall and the other against the hedges on the right side.

The charge was sounded.

The Earl led the attack on one flank and his son, Lord Compton, on the other. It was a complete success, for, no sooner did the bodies of ambushed musketeers see the waves of steel advancing and they heard the thunder of hoofs, than they turned and fled, only to be ridden down and slain on the frosty ground. The two parts then reformed and turned in on the vast square in the centre composed of Brereton's cannon, artillery and musketeers.

A terrible hand to hand fight ensued, lasting for about an hour. Some troops got detached from the rest while they were hunting out bodies of pikemen and musketeers who had retired among the broken ground near Salt.

Brereton commenced to retreat in confusion, leaving his artillery behind, pursued by the victorious right wing of the royalists regardless of all order. This was unfortunate, because the left wing, who had attacked the wall, had lost many in storming it. The Roundhead musketeers had stood firmer behind the brick wall and had taken much life before being driven back.

The one part of the royalists had left the second part of their comrades in such sorry straits that Brereton's men were returning to rescue some of their cannon.

Now Sir John Gell saw his chance, and, with his reserve, pre-pared to charge the reserve of Sir Thomas Byron, and break through to Stafford.

This was the great moment ; as the grey dull of the late Sunday afternoon deepened there came the great charge of horse against horse—the two reserves met in one terrible crash.   Sword crashed on helmet, butt-ends of pistols served as clubs.   Shouts of '' Queen Mary '' came from the Royalists.   '' God, God,'' came from the hoarse throats of the Roundheads, terminating in frightful shrieks.   As soon as the pursuing cavaliers saw the final issue they reformed on the sloping outskirts of the heath and charged into the general mêlee.

That hindered the success of Gell's charge ; they wavered, broke, and fled, leaving the victorious Royalists in possession of the field as night came on, making pursuit impossible, even had   the Royalists been in a position to do so.   For their losses had been heavy, and many had yet to learn that their brave commander had been killed.   If happened after the first charge of the day ; the Earl had reformed his men, in good order, and charged the enemy's centre. The charge was so good and completely successful that they were cutting right through, when the Earl's horse was killed under him. His men swept on leaving the Earl at the mercy of the Roundheads. Though dismounted he immediately pole-axed a Colonel of the Foot and went for a Captain.

His men, unknowing his plight, leaderless now, and the junior officers with their several troops got further away from each other, pursuing different bodies of the flying enemy.   There appeared to be no second in command to take the Earl's place.   The gallant soldier at that moment was surrounded by Roundheads and fighting for his life.   His helmet was knocked off and he was recognised.   Quarter was immediately offered him, but his answer came as strong as his arm : '' A Northampton scorns to take quarter from such base rogues as you.''   He was immediately slain and carried off in Brereton's retreat.

Lord Compton, the Earl's son, who commanded the second part, also received a wound in the leg which made it difficult for him to keep his troops in order, and allowed them to pursue stray parties, instead of reforming and helping their comrades.

Sir Thomas Byron deserves most of the credit for the victory, for he held steady throughout, waiting his chance (and it came in the end) to fly at Gell, when that worthy was charging the raging mass in the centre.

Byron was ordinarily commander of the Prince's Regiment in the Royalist Army, and was highly esteemed for his soldierly qualities. Unfortunately he was also so wounded during his victorious charge that he had to be taken, after the rout, to a near-side cottage for medical attention.

It was a mournful victory that the Royalists had won, for their kind, generous, and noble leader was dead.

They were mostly Warwickshire men that composed his forces; men who had known him all their lives ; friends and tenants. Even two younger sons (Lord Compton was one) had charged with their father into that deadly fray.

Other officers had been wounded in the fight, and the troops sorted themselves out, as night descended upon them as a mantle. Orders were given for fires to be lit, troops to encamp on the heath, wounded dressed, horses picketed, and the roll called. Lord Compton had the field searched for the body of his father, and collected together the baggage, colours, arms, ammunition, with what guns the Round-heads had not tipped into the icy Hopton Pools, where they are supposed to be unto this day.

Daybreak came, with not an enemy to be seen. They had had enough, Brereton had returned to his headquarters at Nant-wich. But for the death of the Earl it would have been a very glorious victory. Many stray horses that had belonged to both sides were found standing by the horse lines and caught.

The Royalists began to bury their dead, and Lord Compton sent a file of horse with a flag of truce after the enemy asking for his father's body. This request was refused, as they would only consider it if the spoils of victory were returned to them, and no Royalist would agree to that.

The whole of the equipment was now made complete, the wounded sent on into Stafford, and the new Lord Northampton with the troops followed. There he wrote a letter to his mother acquainting her of his father's death and his great but mournful end. Many of the dead were interred by the parish of Weston in a nameless grave in the church yard, and the spot is still shown to this day.

One soldier was cut down near Sandon and was interred in the church ; the record in the Parish Register reads :

" John F. Marshall, a soldier mortally wounded at the Battle of Hopton. Dy'd in this Pr'sh and was buryd March 20th, 1642."

The same night one notices, but the recorder had made a mis-take of a year in his entry. An entry in the Uttoxeter records reads :

To a prisoner who came from Hopton Heath, 4d.

Also the following :—

Paid for match-powder, candles, bullets, and coals for some of the town ends, March, 1643, £2 10s. 9d.

Uttoxeter Chronicle.

A portion of the Roundhead forces passed through Milwich in the retreat, and stragglers attempted to loot the church plate Struggles followed between them and the churchwardens, in which the chalice was dented, and the scene ended in the stragglers being worsted. The chalice, from then, was hidden in the village, until the Restoration.

The largest grave that is known, is located in a wood high above Salt Station, and is picked out by a circle of trees, some now

dead and cut down and only the stumps remaining ; the rest flourish
still. The circle is about two feet higher than the general level of the
woods and quite flat, and is covered by multitudes of dead leaves and
bracken, making a soft and springy surface, while here and there a
rotting branch and dry twigs crackle beneath the foot—a great silent
grave. The grave is 16 yards in diameter, while further down the
hill is a small cave overlooking the valley wherein falls a tiny streamlet
with ever-lasting melody.

It is rumoured that some of the cannon were mounted near here,
but this is doubtful.

To this account may be added the following extracts from Stafford records, which throw many interesting sidelights on the battle
and the subsequent days that followed :—

Pd.	W. Harding for going twice to Hampton, himself and his horse, being forth 5 daies and 3 nights when the Earl of Chesterfield and his horses were there	0	11	0
Pd.	Mr. Baddock for going twice to Wolverp'ton	0	5	0
Pd.	for 3 quire paper for Gen. Hastings ...	0	1	6
Pd.	for a sheet to wind a prisoner in	0	0	8
Pd.	for charges bestowed upon a sick Parliament prisoner	0	3	2
Pd.	for a messenger carrying letters unto Sir Richard Leveson, Mr. Broughton, and o'r Justices	0	2	6
	Given Sir W. Brereton's Trumpeters ...	0	2	6
Pd.	for ale and spice bestowed on S. W. Brereton 4 gallons were bestowed on Gen. Hastings. 3 men watched on the steeple during a fast day, also for the town soldiers, ale. 1s. to Committee Porter; messenger a 1s. for bringing letters from Coventry by Capt. Foxall's direction, carriers followed with arms and ammunition, lead used about Greengate. Given two gentlemen that were hurt on Salt Heath, at the request of Major Greene and Capt. Lane	0	2	6
		0	5	0
Pd.	for wine and sugar bestowed on Lord Pagett	0	12	0
Pd.	for Coals and Candles to all Guards, lockes to the Gates, messengers to carry warrants, and some other occasions	11	11	3

Six strike of oats at Sir W. Brereton's coming
in, when the town was taken.
Bestowed in Wine, Sugar, and Sack to Earle
of Denbyth and his Companions at times ...   1—4 0

1643   To a poor man y't was plundered and hurt by
cavaliers as did truly appear 0 1 4

Note.—Armour from Hopton Heath was sent by the Commonwealth
Government to Stafford as a gift, and placed in the Council
Chamber.

THE NOVEMBER ASSIZES AT STAFFORD.

Country-man : What mummery is this ? 'Tis fit only for Guisers.
Townsman : No mummery, sir. 'Tis the Stafford Assizes.

A freezing Wednesday afternoon in November saw me again
travelling to Stafford, and I was greatly looking forward to meeting
again the hospitable friends I had made there.

My compartment, located in the centre of the train, came to a
standstill almost immediately opposite to the station exit, and, gathering
my traps, I prepared to alight. As I hailed a porter an immaculate
young man in morning dress caught my eye. He was emerging from
the next coach. He was busily engaged in fitting what appeared
to be two halves of a wand or cane together, while several similarily
dressed gentlemen, who had been waiting on the platform, marched up
to the door of the compartment and ranged themselves in a line.

Near by hovered the Stationmaster wearing his silk hat*

My curiosity was aroused. What was this strange ceremony
on a railway station that was about to take place ?

Out of the carriage jumps a little man with large hands, with a
shiny silk hat on his head, and a jolly smile on his lined face ; he
raises his hat to the bowing gentlemen in front, and shakes hands with
each, they all bending humbly over his hand as they shake.

The gentleman has apparently no luggage, for he follows his
immaculate young friend with the wand to the exit. I could hear some
bells ringing as I watched, and decided to gratify my curiosity by
asking the ticket collector who the little man was. I knew he must
know him, for I noticed particularly that the little man presented
no ticket as he passed the barrier—probably he had a season ticket.
Beyond I could see more gentlemen, with white wands, and, at that
moment, a trumpeter opposite to them, in uniform, whom I had not
previously observed sounded what appeared like a salute of some
sort.

The little man, indifferent to all this, was hurrying through
the exit to a large car outside as if he was nothing to do with it all

*Only on six stations in England is the privilege accorded to
Stationmasters to wear the traditional silk hat. They formerly carried
a staff and handcuffs.

and the demonstration was for someone else.

The car rolled away with a chauffeur and footman seated in front. Both wore elaborate cockades on their caps.

I questioned the ticket collector.

"Oh, 'im, sir. 'E may be little, sir, but bless you, he's all there. That's the Lord Chief Justice of England, sir, on circuit," said the collector, proudly. " Carn't you 'ear the bells ringing ?"

" Of course, the Assizes, I ought to have known. Thank you very much." Now being enlightened, I took a taxi to the Swan, feeling glad that I was in Stafford on such an important occasion in its life.

Now the Assizes in Stafford are amongst its most ancient institutions and have taken place here for hundreds of years. The name originally meant a sitting to fix prices or assess taxes. There has also been an Assize of Arms, and an Assize of Bread as well as an Assize of Law and an Assize of Clarendon.

The Assembly of Clarendon in the reign of Henry II. first placed litigation and the administration of the law on its proper basis.

It was enacted that, in all suits in the King's Chamber or before the Justices in Eyre, for the recovery of land, if a tenant declined trial by combat he might put himself on the " Assize." This consisted of four Knights and twelve others chosen by the Sheriff, and by the verdict of the sixteen the cause was decided..

This was based on the Anglo-Saxon system, in use before the Norman Conquest, and resembles the modern trial by jury.

Justices, who were mostly priests, were first created in 1118, and were regularly appointed by the King's Chamber. The Assize of Clarendon was confirmed by the Common Council of the Realm at Northampton, and a new arrangement made of sending Justices on Circuit. These were called Justices in Eyre, or itinerant Justices, and they went on Circuit once in seven years. The country was divided into six Circuits, to each of which three Justices were appointed.

From this the modern Assizes sprang, and instead of six circuits they are in the teens, Staffordshire being in the Oxford Circuit, and the Judges came three times a year, Summer, Autumn, and Winter, instead of once in seven years.

The Council meeting at Clarendon, near Salisbury, 1164, was composed of prelates and barons, and was under the presidency of John, Bishop of Oxford. These constitutions were the cause of the split between Henry II. and Thomas à Beckett, who refused to observe them, and partially the cause of his murder.

One provision was that every ecclesiastic accused of a crime should be tried in the civil courts, and mandates like this naturally

*The office of Lord Chief Justice was created by Henry II. with the title of Chief Justiciar. This was the highest office of the State and the holder of it was the King's deputy in the Judicial Court. He is now only the head of the Court of King's Bench.

roused Beckett's opposition, he being a staunch champion of the church, and its then enormous privileges.

So that since the year 1118 there have been (though perhaps in its earliest institution very irregular), visitations of the Judges on Circuit ; the need growing as the country gained benefit from the decisions of the law, for more frequent visits, until Justices came once a year, and later on three times, as at present.

We hear of the Assize in the reign of Edward II. :—
" John de Charnes, in company with Roger de Swynnerton, Nicholas de Swynnerton, Rector of Muccleston, and several others, held up His Majesty's Judges of Assize, then sitting at Clifton Campville,* Staffs., and prevented them from doing their business."

It seems that there was some indictment being tried, of which some of these gentlemen were the subject, and so they resented it. They overawed the court by the presence of a large body of their retainers, armed to the teeth, terrorised the witnesses, fined the jurymen, fined the Coroner still more, and then decamped.

We wonder where the Sheriff and his javelin men were on this exciting occasion.

In the year 1558, in the latter days of Queen Mary's reign, is the first mention of the Assizes being held at Stafford. In that year a Bill for the purpose of holding a county assize was introduced into Parliament in March. It will be of interest to recall a local case of the propitiation of a judge by the present of a sugar loaf.* From Corporation accounts :

1621 Pd Mr. Maye for a sugar loaf bestowed on Justice Warburton at Summer Assizes, when we conferred with him for the wrong done unto us about indictments performed at the Assizes, tendinge to the breach of our liberties.

1633 Pd W. Donnington for his house for the Judges at Assizes, £1.
1636   For altering and taking down and setting up the Checker at the Assizes, according to the Judge's directions.

In 1575 Queen Elizabeth came to Stafford in her progress through Staffordshire, coming from Chartley, where she had been staying. Her keen eyes, noticing the town had not been flourishing, asked the Bailiffs the cause.

They replied that the reason was the decay of the capping trade, and also that the Assizes had been taken away from the town. " To the wch, her Matie lovinglie answered that she would renew and establish better the said statute for Cappinge, and for the Assizes shee gave her pmise that the same should be ever after be kept at Stafford."

*Note.—From A.D. 1199 the Assizes were often held at Lichfield.

*Cane sugar moulded into a conical lump, usually weighing about 24 lbs.

The Judges' Porter and the Judges' Crier also attended at Assize to add majesty to the proceedings. The Chaplain received a bottle of wine.

The Queen did not prevent the new fashions from killing the old, and this has happened in other days besides hers, when queens have tried to make fashion change. The Assizes, owing to her kindness, were ordered to be kept here for evermore.

This was admirably portrayed in the Elizabethan scene in the Millenary Pageant of 1913, when Stafford celebrated its 1,000 years existence.

Extracts from Stafford Millenary Pageant, 1913.

Gillian : The trumpets, Madge ! They come.
Cicely : Oh, how I long to see the goodly Queen !
The sour-faced man (to himself): The foolish lasses !

> (To blare of trumpets and cheering enter
> Royal procession, escorted by Bailiffs).

Herald : Who holdeth her Majesty's stirrup ?
Lord Stafford : I, Lord Stafford, do so in virtue of my tenure of Coton.

> Queen and others dismount, and are led to dais.
> Horses led off by pages).

	Queen.	
Court.		Court.
Corporation.		Corporation.
Crowd.		Crowd.

Bailiffs present cups.

First Bailiff : We beseech your Majesty graciously to accept from your Majesty's right loving subjects of Stafford these cups, twin symbols of our love and loyalty.

Queen (graciously accepting them): Alas, poor souls, other towns give us of their wealth, but you give us of your want. Now, say, if you can devise in any maner waie, how we may do you good ?

First Bailiff : In truth your Majesty's gracious desire to further us is already accomplished. As the sun dispels the mist—so in the glory of your Majesty's presence——

Queen : As for our presence, 'tis here but for a day. More lasting *presents*, methinks, were what ye lack. Speak, now, and we will further you.

Second Bailiff (eagerly): 'Tis the trade, your Majesty. Alas, our cloth caps are out of fashion, and the cap-makers stand idle.

Queen (signing Courtier nearer): So—'tis a case of " doublet from Italy, round hose from France, and bonnet from Germany," eh ? (Looking round) Gentlemen—the Stafford cap must come to Court.

> (Laughter from Courtiers, who acquiesce, and cheers from crowd).

First Bailiff : And also, your Majesty—for that the Assizes be taken away from the town.

Queen : Then the Assizes must e'en come back, and be held here for ever.

Robert Sutton (advancing with Burgesses, presents petition):

We, the Clerk of St. Mary's Church, and burgesses of Stafford, do beg to present to your gracious Majesty this petition——

Queen (alarmed at length) : What is't, what is't, good Master Clerk ?

Clerk : For want of the revenue lost to the town in the reign of his Majesty King Edward VI. the services of the Church suffer—no Rector has been appointed—the which is most grievous.

Queen : And ye are the Church's Clerk. Then be ye Rector—and let St. Mary's be the Parish Church and so continue. And see to it that ye bring all the citizens to Church, Sir Rector.

Burgess : And the monies, your Majesty ?

Queen : Ah, our Royal brother forgot to restore the revenues ? Then must we do a tardy repentance. (To Chancellor) See ye to it. (To burgess) And see that you pay our worthy Master Rector here a goodly sum.

(Bailiffs present Maces to her Majesty again, who delivers them again).

A curious thing is that a bill was passed through the House of Lords three years before for the keeping of the Assize at Stafford. This did not appear to have been put into operation.

In 1798 the new Shire Hall was commenced in the Market Square and during this time, the Assizes were held in the nave of St. Mary's Church, it being of course the only other place of sufficient size in the town. This may seem rather strange, to hold an Assize in such a place, but, in early days, churches had many other uses, besides being a house of religion. It was even sometimes a strong place of safety to be held in emergency as a fort, while a look-out for enemies was kept from its embattled tower ; its church-yard was used for games and exercises, and in some places the theatrical properties of the mummers were kept in it ;* so worshippers, when they occupy their pews at St. Mary's on Sunday mornings, little realise that their beloved edifice has echoed the dread sentence of death from the lips of the shrouded judge in days long passed by. Valuable possessions were often stored in it, and civilly, as well as religiously, it meant far more to our forebears than it may mean to us to-day. So no one would see any harm in justice being administered in its precincts. The assize would, no doubt, open as it does now, with a service in the chancel, after which the procession would proceed to the nave for the legal business, with all reverence and respect.

Extract from the Corporation Accounts concerning the Assizes, 27th March, 1691.

'' Whereas there has been £20 allowed yearly towards the charges of the Judges, and the late Sheriffs have not paid the same to the Mayor then in being : it is ordered that Mr. Mayor do appoint

*e.g., at Abbott's Bromley the properties of the Horn Dancers are kept in the Church to this day.

some persons to inspect into the accounts of the late Sheriffs and to see what has been allowed them for the entertainment of the Judges, and to demand such allowances from the said Sheriffs : and in case the Sheriffs shall refuse to pay the same, then such course to be taken for the getting thereof as shall be thought fit, and that the same money when gotten to be applyed to that use."

To that effect an order was made to " pay £2 2s. to every under sheriff when he bring £20 for the Judges' charges."

Seven years later :

" Sheriff's horses for the use of Justices were allowed a peck of beans and peas to mix with 2 strikes of oats, and that saddle horses be allowed a peck a day, but a peck and a half a day for every coach horse. The Chamberlain to take account of all."

Two dozen bottles of wine were also presented to the Judges, but this gift was ended when their salaries were raised.

THE LAW COURTS IN THE SHIRE HALL.

" The strains of the organ reach the crowd as they wait,
To feast eyes on his Lordship at the Church-yard gate ;
First come the tip-staves and trumpeter small,
Followed by Ushers, in top hats so tall.
A pause—then Sheriff in silver and mauve,
Preceded by Chaplain, awes all in the Grove ;
Behind comes the Marshall, with wand in hand,
Who hastens to join the waiting band.
Then next out comes the Judge, as the boys cease to sing ;
To the law courts, to judge whether the guilty shall swing."

—D.W.

Next morning I breakfasted in company with a barrister, who had arrived about the same time yesterday as I had, and we struck up an acquaintance in the bar that night. I was looking at a local paper, ' The Staffordshire Advertiser,'' dated the previous Saturday, when, on the front page, the following notice caught my eye :

STAFFORDSHIRE AUTUMN ASSIZES, 1930.

Notice is hereby given that an ASSIZE will be held at STAFFORD, in and for the County of Stafford, on WEDNESDAY, the 19th day of NOVEMBER, 1930. The Business of the said Assize will commence on THURSDAY, the 20th of NOVEMBER, at the SHIRE HALL in STAFFORD, when the Trial of Prisoners will be forthwith commenced, at Eleven o'clock in the Forenoon, at which time and place all Justices of the Peace, Mayors, Coroners, Escheators, Stewards, and also all Chief Constables and Bailiffs of every Hundred and Liberty, and also all Prosecutors, Witnesses, Solicitors, and all Jurors summoned for that day must attend.

Dated this 1st day of NOVEMBER, 1930.

RICHARD FOWLER BUTLER, High Sheriff.
Sheriff's Office, Stafford.

I pointed this out to my legal friend, and I remarked on the quaint phraseology.

" Yes, very," he replied.   ' ' Have you seen the calendar for this Assize ?"

" Calendar—Calendar !   I'm afraid I do not understand."

" Oh, the list of cases with the Indictments," he said, smilingly. At this he handed a document over to me headed :

The Calendar of Assize and General Gaol Delivery,
etc., etc.

A list of indictments followed—one of the most miscellaneous that any two Judges could be called to sit in judgment on.   Some crimes, however, were of so horrible a character that they seem to defile our boasted civilisation.   So terrible that the press would not even print a syllable, and, as I read on to the end I felt that if there was any indictment for cannibalism I should not have been surprised —even a case of Black Magic was entered.

I handed back the Calendar, and the barrister rose to go, saying he must go down to the Station Hotel where most of his brethren were staying, on some business for that day.

A little later I strolled out into the foggy street, in the direction of the Market Square, just in time to see the Judges' Procession starting out for the Judges' Service at St. Mary's.   At the head of it walked a Police Inspector, with waxed moustache and sword belt, motioning the oncoming traffic to a standstill.   A posse of police followed him, carrying curious great staves with massive heads and an inscription wound round.

The eight police officers that precede the Judge in this singular manner take the place of the old Javelin men, who were provided by the Sheriff to guard the Judge before the days of the police.

Six of them, two by two, march ponderously along bearing their staves that represent the old javelins.   Those on the right carry the staves in their right hands, the left row bear the staves in their left hands.   This is a most interesting relic of the days when the Judges' guards crossed their weapons to keep back the rabble while their Lord-ships passed.   The custom has been handed down to the present and the meaning almost lost ; even the Police do not know why they carry them thus.

Now the two remaining police officers who march at the rear of the Sheriff's car are singularly enough weaponless.

Here is another interesting survival.   The javelin men were gradually reduced for reasons of expense to only two.   They were then mounted like footmen behind the coach, until they, too, were done away with.   Cars came in fashion and it was now impossible for two mounted policemen to be mounted behind, so they now walk near to the position where their picturesque predecessors once rode.

They were followed by silk-hatted Councillors, with the Sergeant of Mace, in his livery, bearing the Mace in front of the Mayor, who, in his robes and chain of office, and bearing a wand in his white-gloved hand, walked with his Deputy, and the tall, bewigged Town Clerk walked beside him. Two ushers, with wands, came next, and then the Trumpeter in a blue uniform with the broad red piping of the Artillery, with his gleaming trumpet, with its gorgeous banner of black and amber. The Under-Sheriff followed, bearing a wand with a silver acorn at the apex.

Then, out of the fog, rolled the huge car conveying the two Judges, with the High Sheriff and his Chaplain, while two policemen, more pompous and awe inspiring, walked on either side, as already mentioned.

I followed the procession as it wended its way up St. Mary's Lane, where, at the Church Gate, the Judges' Marshall was waiting with his thin wand.

The Marshall always precedes the Judges' procession to St. Mary's Church at the opening of the Assize, sees all is in readiness at the Church, and then awaits their Lordships at the gates, bearing his wand of office. An equerry performs the same service when the King attends Divine Service.

The car stopped, and the cockaded footman, riding with the chauffeur, sprang out and ran round, to open the door as the trumpeter poured out his salute.

First came the Chaplain, and then the High Sheriff in his court dress, with a huge flash on his back and a magnificent sword girded at his side, got out, and, removing his hat, helped the Lord Chief Justice in his robes to alight. I hardly recognised him as the funny little man I had seen the day before. He was accompanied by a Commissioner more than twice as tall, who must have arrived at a different time, for I had not seen him before.

The choir and clergy, who had been waiting for their arrival, now turned, and to the strains of the organ, began to perambulate the nave to the Chetwynd pew, followed by the Churchwardens, with their staffs,* and the rest of the procession, the two learned brothers, rather odd in the difference of stature between them, bringing up the rear.

The Chetwynd pew in St. Mary's Church is the official seat of the Mayor of Stafford during his year of office, being originally the family pew of the Chetwynds of Chetwynd House. It consists of three seats, with comfortable arms, and a rest at the end, to which the Mace-bearer advanced and fixed the mace to show the seat of authority to all beholders. The Mayor, Sheriff, etc., all waited at this pew for the two Judges, who very slowly were solemnly pacing up the nave.

On taking their seats, the Sheriff took his, and the Mayor and officials occupied the Corporation pews behind, while the Rector

*In days past the wardens paraded the aisles carrying long rods. Immediately a nodding head was seen down would come the rod with a smart tap, and only rarely was it necessary to repeat the punishment.

escorted the Chaplain up into the chancel to the ecclesiastical seats of the mighty.

I crept into a seat near a beautiful font, the figures of which intrigued me very much, and, as the Sheriff's Chaplain read the lessons, '' And you shall pray for the learned counsels of our Sovereign Lord the King, that they may be faithful to the Christian injunction of the Apostle Paul, ' Judge nothing until God brings to light hidden things of darkness and makes manifest the counsels of the heart ' ''—I tried to decipher the inscription.

I afterwards discovered that it was probably brought from the Holy Land during the Crusades, and its origin and inscriptions are the subject of much controversy. At the base are quaint carvings of lions with two inscriptions ; one round the base :

Discretvs non, HS. Q: Non Fvgis ; Ecce Leones,

and is supposed to translate to :

Unwise you be, who do not flee ; the lions see.

Inscription of upper part, with some words missing :

Tv De Jerusalem

Roi ——————— alem

Me Facians Talem

Tam Pvlchrvm Tam Specialem

and supposed by some to be an address from some knightly donor, reading :

Mayst thou from Salem (such my prayer),

Triumphal booty homeward bear, because thou this hast made me wear a form so beautiful, so rare !

This font is the oldest work in the Church, with a cavity big enough for the complete immersion of an infant.

Another quaint feature of St. Mary's is an old lantern formerly used by the ringers to light their way up to the belfry.

I thought of Izaak Walton, yonder in his niche with the carved rushes beneath the bust. He would be baptised here, in this mysterious font ; how nice for the members of this church to feel that they had been baptised at this same gateway in the Church of God.

The service was now finishing, and to the sound of the closing hymn, the Crucifer, holding his cross on high, led the way to the great south door, with its giant hinges. They should go to the west door really on such occasions. Both Judges paused here to shake hands with the bowing clergy, and proceeded solemnly to the car.

I leisurely followed them down the Lane, and admired, as I went, the overhanging storeys of the Ancient High House, the highest projecting portion being six feet out of the perpendicular, and thought what a shelter it must be on a wet day. The inscription recording the visit of King Charles faces this lane, with numbers of small hooks underneath in lines.

I am told that with all the modern traffic, which is particularly heavy here, the main street being a bottle neck, the overhang never increases a fraction of an inch.

It was assuredly picturesque, and rich enough in elaborate architectural detail. What a fine facade it presents, high roof, quaint gables, huge chimneys, and bay windows full of leaded panes, one window with bars showing its former use as a nursery.

As I reached the Market Square, full of parked cars and crowds of people, the trumpeter had detached himself from the procession, which had wound round to the Judges' Lodgings adjoining the Shire Hall, and, amidst the cars, sounded a call. This call, which announces to all and sundry, that the court is about to sit, is known as the Sheriff's Fanfare, and has descended from trumpeter to trumpeter. It has never been committed to paper.

The present Assize Trumpeter is an Artillery man, and he also acts at the Quarter Sessions. A previous holder of the office wore a gold laced hat and livery,, and carried a silver trumpet with an emblazoned banner. The banner was retained by the Sheriff at the conclusion of his Shrievalty, and the trumpet by the trumpeter as his perquisite.

We have divine authority for the calling together of assemblies by the use of trumpets. Moses was commanded by God to make trumpets of silver to call the people to solemn assembly and holy sacrifices.

After the fanfare is sounded the trumpeter marches down to the corner of Martin Street, and coming smartly to attention, repeats it. A short time ago he also went the other way, along Bank Passage, and sounded the call again at the far end near the Vine.

The ancient procedure was, that on the opening of the court, trumpeters should announce it to the four corners of the land. This practice should be followed now. At the conclusion of this perambulation the trumpeter passes into court, to remain in attendance, and I followed him.

It is now meet to make some description of the important hall where the curtain was about to be raised on one of the most solemn scenes, when justice was about to be administered from the leather-swivelled judgment seats of the two courts.

The Shire Hall is part of an enormous block of buildings that are the mainspring of the County of Stafford. They consist of the Shire Hall, which fronts on to the Market Square, with its few plane and chesnut trees, and extends down Market Street, where is the witnesses' entrance, and the disused turn-stile where the prisoners were formerly '' checked '' through the gateway into the court yard, where the chief gaoler receives the general gaol delivery. Adjoining is the house of the custodian of the hall, and next the Rose and Crown Inn, cheek by jowl with the Borough Hall, with its various municipal buildings fronting Eastgate Street.

The Chief Constable's House,* with its old oak panelling, dormer windows, and offices, skirts Martin Street ; and here join the

*A collection of implements used by convicted felons is located here, and constitutes a miniature '' Chamber of Horrors.''

County Buildings, with its Council Chamber, built as a replica of the House of Lords, and then the Judges' Lodgings in St. Martin's Place, with a wide space in front where the Sheriff's coach and four used to turn in, again links up, and directly communicates with the Shire Hall.

The Shire Hall was built in 1798-9 with a stone front with four Doric semi-cloumns in the front, where two figures, on which pigeons often rest, hold the scales of justice and the Sword of Mercy. The intervening space is occupied by a clock.

The interior consists of a fine assembly room with handsome columns, usually used for badminton and General Elections, and beyond, a staircase leading underground, on the right being the Crown Court and on the left the Nisi Prius Court, while a multitude of rooms serve for Grand Jury room, robing room, clerk of indictments room, jury room, etc.

Downstairs leads to the cells, where a labyrinth of torturous passages communicate with the two courts above, and the "condemned cells" to which convicted murderers are brought, sometimes shrieking and sometimes carried senseless until their removal, and a mass of old cellars that belonged to the original county hall, and are very ancient. In some one can see where the torches scorched the wall with their flames as they illuminated the huddled prisoners in their chains—men, women and children all herded together.

In one place a great mass of bundled documents, forgotten evidence, is piled high up, some in boxes, much loose, and the whole covered by years of dust and dirt.

Among the quaint customs carried out during the Assize is the picketing of two policemen, one outside the Judge's House, and one along the passage at the back of the Crown Court.

Supposing the first officer were asked what he was there for he would reply that he was guarding the Judges' House. The first officer is taken off duty as soon as the Judge passes into his lodgings ; so apparently the Judge and lodgings are left to take care of themselves. The reason is that there is a little known entrance into the court on that side, although neither the officer or anyone else now knows it. The second constable patrolling the passage has still less notion of his use ; those who place him there do not know why they station him there. The reason is lost; he is like the sentry that a Russian Czar placed years ago to guard a wild flower blooming in his park, to please his lady. The flower faded, but still, year after year, a sentry was still mounted in that same spot, although flower, Czar, lady, and the reason were all gone.

Such was the building in which I found myself, and in which grim scenes were about to be enacted, and wandering up the stairs into the vestibule opposite the Grand Jury room, all the doors being

Note.—The Town Chamberlain proclaimed the Assize in the town.

Note.—The Assizes always open with the Norman French prolomation of Oyez, Oyez, Oyez.

guarded, I saw my friend the barrister. Knowing my errand, he bid me come on tip-toe along the passage to the left, past a curtained doorway and he paused at the end. '' Just inside, on the left,'' he whispered, and holding up his hand for silence, pushed me in.

I found myself sitting on a bench, next to the Chaplain, whom I had heard read the Lesson in St. Mary's earlier that morning. The Sheriff was sitting by the Lord Chief Justice, who was, at that moment, reading his charge to the Grand Jury, who were seated in two rows on my right. On the other side of the Judge were his Marshall and Clerk and the Mayor. I noticed there were no barristers in court, and presently the Grand Jury filed out to consider whether to return true bills or not.

While they were gone I had time to take notice of my surroundings. The court was octagonal in shape, and much smaller than I expected, with the dock in the centre and the public gallery rising up, crowded with people, and crowned by a fine portrait in oils hanging on the wall behind.

In this gallery were two policemen with very long canes, 18ft. long, for tapping the heads of any unruly members of the public. On the left was the jury box, with the witness box between that and the bench.

The well of the court was occupied by the solicitors' table, benches for reporters and the official shorthand writer, while on the wall above the police superintendent's box, was a bust of Justice Talfourd, who was taken ill on the judgment seat and died while on the Assize at Stafford. He was the original of Traddles in David Copperfield, and was seized with apoplexy while the court was sitting.

Mr. Justice Talfourd, to whom Charles Dickens dedicated that immortal work, Pickwick Papers, passed away in a moment, with words of Christian eloquence and of brotherly tenderness and kindness to all men, yet unfinished, on his lips. John Forster describes him as '' facile and fluent of the kindliest speech.'' He was said to have assumed nothing with the ermine except a desire for more friendship with those he loved, and was one of the best friends Charles Dickens ever had, and before his elevation to the bench, when he was Sergeant at Law, was briefed by him (Dickens) to put a stop to the piracy of his works.

We read of him in David Copperfield, as Tommy Traddles, in a tight sky-blue suit that made his arms and legs like German sausages —roly-poly puddings—he was the merriest and most miserable of boys. He was always being caned and was always going to write to his uncle about it, and never did. After laying his head on the desk for a little while he would cheer up somehow, begin to laugh again and draw skeletons all over his slate, before his eyes were dry.

I used at first to wonder what Traddles found in drawing skeletons, and for some time looked upon him as a sort of hermit, who reminded himself by those symbols of mortality, that caning couldn't last for ever.

But I believe it was because they were easy, and didn't want any features !

Sir Thomas Noon Talfourd, judge and poet, friend and biographer of Charles Lamb, died in this sudden manner in 1854.

The dock on which my attention was now focussed was surrounded by spiked bars, partially covered with a curtain, and it had in it desks for the chief warder and doctor, between which ran a staircase that communicated with the cells beneath. The space left for the prisoner was at a small table in front, directly facing the Judge and the Clerk of Assize, who sits beneath him.

One can appreciate, when sitting in the Crown Court, that absolute silence is necessary, both from within and without, in order that the often almost whispered words of witnesses, judges, and prisoners can be heard. The quietness in which evidence is given, cross examination is conducted, and the almost inaudible replies of witnesses, all help to give a feeling of solemnity. Many of the replies can only just be heard by, what one would describe, as the inner circle of the court, consisting of the Judge, jury, barristers, press and prisoner, and the all-important official shorthand writer.

No one else can scarcely hear a word, and the gallery most of the time sits in ignorance of what is passing. It is very surprising to the uninitiated, how rivetted one's attention must be, even in the inner circle, to gather all that is said.

The Judge is the only one that fidgets on the judgment seat, and pulls his wig, rustles his papers, closes his eyes, in fact, does everything but look at the prisoner.

All know that these are the only outward signs that he is keenly concentrated on the case as it unfolds like a romance, simple or sinister, and only now and then is the trend of his mind shown when something of moment arises which causes an interjection from him. It may be only to inquire what '' carriage-forward '' may mean, or '' what a door standing ajar '' may infer. The question is asked in a languid manner, followed by a frown as a titter sweeps over the gallery, and policemen tap offenders with their tall wands, and pompous ushers shout '' Silence '' in stentorious voices.

Simple questions like these are often asked by judges, not because they do not know themselves, but perhaps some of the members of the jury may not know, and it is their delicate way of putting them wise.

Many judges are jokingly said to come down in the world when they assume the ermine, because when young barristers they always must dress very correctly and expensively, but, as judges, they can wear any old ragged coat under their gorgeous robes, and no one would know. Also, when young and briefless, their rooms are nearly

Note.—'' Dock '' is an old Flemish word meaning a cage, and in ancient days the dock was an actual cage, made of iron bars, and protected by horrible spikes. Similar spikes still embellish the dock in the Crown Court but they are partly concealed by a curtain.

always at the top of a building, but when they take " silk " they descend to the first floor. They have very great learning, derived from many channels, but like many lawyers, have rather a dictatorial " ensemble." Their make-up would be better if it included the finesse of the level-headed business man.

As for juries, particularly common juries, being drawn from all walks of life, and therefore containing all the elements of the English mind, the one amazing thing about them is that they are not paid, only in certain cases. Surely the services of any juryman are worth £1 1s. a day, not as payment, but just as a gentle acknowledgment, not because he has to do this duty, as he would do that in any case, but just as a Freeman's fee. All labourers in the fields of justice are worthy of their hire.

At one time the Salt Library was always closed during the time the Assizes are being held, as it contains the Statutes of England, Pipe Rolls, and many legal works of reference, preserved in its archives, and thus the whole was placed at the immediate service of the Courts, should their use be necessary.

On the day before the Assize opens, and continuing until they close, the general post office in Stafford, as in all other Assize towns, specially stocks judicature fee stamps for the convenience of the Law Courts. For their greater convenience these stamps can be obtained outside the regular hours for stamps.

The solicitors' seats are on both sides of the dock. This renders consultations easy between them and the prisoner at the bar.

I wondered what the feelings of a murderer would be after the months of waiting in prison, after the dreary coroner's court, the magistrates' court, and now to be brought along dark passages, shoved up some steps into the bright light of the court, face to face with the man whose duty it will be to try him, without fear or favour.

Now the Grand Jury have returned and the Judge comes in to hear their unanimous verdict of true bills in all cases ; the barristers troop into court ; the common jury is sworn by the Clerk ; and the real business of the trial begins.

Formerly all jurymen, witnesses, and prisoners had to come each day until the case in which they were engaged came on, but now only the jury serving, and the waiting jury, need attend.

All the prisoners are brought the first day in case any of them are required by the Grand Jury, but after that they only come on the day of their trial. This makes the court precincts are not so busy during Assize after the first day.

Shortly afterwards the court adjourned for lunch, and a procession consisting of the Under-Sheriff, with his wand, led the way

Note.—In 1909 Edward Marshall Hall appeared for the defence in what he afterwards called his greatest victory in a murder trial at the Staffordshire Assizes.

along the passage, followed by the Chaplain, carrying his " mortar-board," then the Sheriff preceded the Judge, and the rear was brought up by the Marshall and Clerk.

As they crossed the vestibule leading to the judge's lodgings the staircase door was locked, and the keeper stood with his back against it.

I am told that the door is locked to prevent anyone being in the vestibule while the Judge passes.　The presence of an interested party in one of the cases might mean something to the Judge, and is known as intimidation.

This form is gone through each time the Judge passes during the business of the Assize.

Note.—A barrister's gown still has a fold at the back that represents the original pocket into which his fees were dropped.

Form of Portion of the Calendar of Assize and General Gaol Delivery.

Name.................................... Age............ Date.................
Place.................... Committed............... Remanded..............
Bailed............................... Surrendered.....................
Offence...
Tried before.................................... Date....................
Verdict or Plea...
Sentence or Order of the Court...

THE HIGH SHERIFF AND OTHERS.

" The rich man in his castle,
The poor man at his gate,
God made them high and lowly,
And ordered their estate."

The Office of High Sheriff of Staffordshire is one of the oldest and highest in the County, and is usually held by a County Magistrate, who is also, as a rule, a rich man, as the office entails considerable expenditure during his tenure.

There is a tradition that the Stafford Knot was invented by an early Sheriff, who had only one rope to hang three prisoners by, and another that he had four prisoners to hang, and let the one off who devised the curious knot in which the other three were hanged.

Anyhow, the whole is shrouded in the mists of antiquity, but as there is always some underlying truth in fables, it does show that the Sheriff was about his lawful business even then.

The office of Sheriff was again started by King Henry II. to represent the King in each County, to see that justice was done, and to carry out the law on capital charges.　That part of the exalted office is now performed by the under-Sheriff.

The new Sheriff is nowadays appointed by the Chancellor of the Exchequer, who attends the annual ceremony of the nomination of Sheriffs for England and Wales, which takes place early in November at the Lord Chief Justice's Court in the King's Bench Division. Several Judges sit with the Chancellor, in his black and gold robes, to support him in the annual custom when the nominations are made, from which the King will make his final selection in the time-honoured ceremony of "pricking" the name with a golden bodkin of the new holder of the Shrievalty—a relic of the times when Kings could not write. There are three names put forward from each county for nomination.

He then receives the warrant of his appointment, and, armed with this, appears before a justice of the peace in the county town of the county he represents, there to make a declaration on taking office.

Following is a copy of an old Royal Warrant of the Sheriff's appointment in the reign of George II. :

George the Second by the Grace of God of Great Britain, France and Ireland, King Defender of the faith and so forth, To Archbishops, Bishops, Dukes, Earls, Barons, Knights, freeholders and all others of our County of Stafford ————————————Greetings. Whereas we have committed to our well-beloved Richard Drakeford, of Castle Church, Esquire,—— the custody of our said County with the Appurtenances during our pleasure as by our Letters patent to him thereof made more fully appears   We command you that ye be aiding answering, and assisting to the said Richard Drakeford————as our Sheriff, of our said County in all things while appertaining to the said office.

In Witness whereof we have caused these our Letters to be made patent.

Witness ourself at Westminster the Seventh Day of February in the Twenty-Sixth year of our Reign.

(Great Seal). (Signed) STRANGE MILFORD.

In 1584 Thomas Gresley the High Sheriff, was ordered by Queen Elizabeth to seize household stuff from the attainted Lord Paget's mansion at Beaudesert and convey it to Tutbury for the use Mary Queen of Scots.

In 1674, John Wilson, a vintner of Stafford, was appointed High Sheriff, and arms were granted to him by Sir William Dugdale.

A curious appointment was once made for the year 1807, when a G. Briscoe was pricked. The announcement in the " Advertiser " was as follows :

G. BRISCOE, SUMNELL HILL, ESQ.

" The gentleman who has been appointed High Sheriff for this County is insensible of the honour intended him, having, we are told, ' to the grave gone down,' upwards of two years ago." So much for that.

In Cornwall the writs issued are in a different form to those issued for other Sheriff's of Counties, because the appointment is in the hands of the Prince of Wales acting as Duke of Cornwall.

A similar state of affairs exists in the Palatine Counties. The Sheriff for the County of Lancashire is appointed by the Duke of Lancaster, who happens to be the King, and holds the Duchy.

For some 600 years the crown was actually unable to appoint a Sheriff for the County of Westmoreland at all, because the privilege of being Sheriff of Westmoreland was a hereditary one in the hands of the Clifford and the Tufton families.

The right of being or appointing was given to the Veteriponts by King John.

It descended to two heiresses, Isabella and Idonea, and on the death of Idonea, passed by the marriage of Isabella to the Clifford family. Both Idonea and Isabella are stated to have exercised the office of Sheriff in person.

The privilege remained in the hands of the Cliffords until late Stuart times, coming to Lady Anne Clifford, who also exercised the office in person, and met, received, and entertained the Judges of Assize, preceded them into the County, riding on horseback, and sat on the Bench with them.

When too old to carry out the duties in person she appointed a Deputy-Sheriff to do it for her.

The right of appointment reverted to the Crown in 1849 from the Tufton family, to whom the privilege had descended from the Cliffords : the Tuftons receiving compensation from the Crown for the transfer of the right.

In the archives of the Tuftons are still preserved the original Sheriff's seal, and a long series of documents under the Great Seal, concerning this extraordinary privilege, which they alone of all the families of England possessed.

The Sheriff is, of course, responsible for the entertainment of the Judge in the County on the business of the Assize, to escort him to and from his lodgings, and attend him while the court is sitting. He is usually a Deputy Lieutenant and a wealthy man, and is responsible for the payments to various people connected with the court, such as the Trumpeter and Javelin Men, etc.

Stafford, unfortunately, has no javelin men now, and two of the javelins that they once carried are in the Izaak Walton Cottage at Shallowford. It is a pity that the office is not revived. Meals provided for the Grand Jury, also fall to his lot to pay for.

Note.—The High Sheriff's court dress has a ribbon called a "flash" on the back of the coat collar, which represents the tail of the bagwig, as it lay on the coat.

High Sheriffs have the privilege of appearing in full court dress at the Bar of the House of Commons if they have occasion to present any petition to the House.

Note.—A sheriff's perquisite was the clothes of those condemned to burn.

Some years ago the Sheriff gave a Sheriff's Breakfast, since done away with. If the Sheriff is a soldier he will sometimes wear uniform, and one Sheriff, not long ago appearing in khaki, was ordered to remove his military cap by an irate Judge. He replied that a soldier should not remove his head gear even in the presence of the King. But, anyway, he did, and the Judge told him afterwards that he could have fined him a £100.

Fines, even of officials, are easily incurred at Assize ; Grand Jury can be fined for being late, also the Governor of the Prison if he does not get his prisoners to court in time for the opening, also the Common Jury ; in fact, the Judge has power to take these latter round on circuit with him, for breaches.

The Under-Sheriff, who is either a barrister or a solicitor, deputises for the High Sheriff at executions, and also arranges the legal details connected with the court and looks after the ushers, etc. Well may he be termed Under-Sheriff ! A former Under-Sheriff of one county, after witnessing an execution, would arrange for a trip in an air-plane to restore his nerves.

When a death sentence is due to be carried out the Sheriff of the county has to select the executioner from a list of four men recognised by the Home Office—or he may choose, if he prefers to pay a lower fee, one of several others who have previously acted as assistants.

It is a very ancient appointment. In court he wears morning dress and white gloves, and carries a wand bearing a silver acorn at the apex.

He also presides over cases of compensation returned from the High Court, with a jury to assess damages, etc.

The Judge's Marshall, whose sole legal function is to receive records for trials, and swear in the Grand Jury, is the sole friend and companion of the Judge in his kingly exile when on circuit ; in some cases a Judge's son has been Marshall to his father.

A famous Marshall on this circuit was Judge Parry who was noted for his dexity in carving a chicken, and opening a bottle of soda water.

The Chaplain, who is of course appointed by the Sheriff on taking office, is usually Vicar of the Parish where the Sheriff lives, and, no doubt, obtains much future material for his sermons as he listens to the cases (or ought to). Nothing one can imagine could give anyone a greater knowledge of men and things than to sit in an Assize Court half a dozen times. Another ancient office connected with the Court is the Keeper of the Wine Cellar.

In early days, no doubt, care had to be taken to see that the Judge's wine was not poisoned, and the Keeper of the Wine Cellar would have to personally superintend on occasions when it was de-

Note.—At the Old Bailey in London the Under-Sheriff wears Court dress and sits at the foot of the Judge's table at lunch,

canted. Nowadays, probably, he is only expected to supplement the supply. The Judge's wine cellar was, curiously enough, located under Messrs. Thorns, the Ironmongers, in Gaolgate, it being only recently that it was removed to the cellars under the Judge's House. There was, it is said, some Jubilee port, of great excellence, put down to celebrate that event. There is also a Circuit Butler and Bailiff.

The Chaplain's only legal function is to say " Amen " at the conclusion of the " Death Sentence," and the allusion to this solemn ceremony make one remember the Black Cap, arranged by the Clerk on the head of the presiding Judge.

The origin of the Black Cap is connected with the ancient days when Judges were usually clerics, and the two offices had not been separated. All members of the clerical order had the crown of the head shaved, and this was called a tonsure, as a sign of initiation into Holy Orders. The bare patch on a judge's or barrister's wig is a remnant of the tonsure, and it is this tonsure that the judge covers with a black cap while passing a sentence of death. It shows, that for the time being, he lays aside his clerical office, it being against the primitive canons for a churchman to have anything to do with the death of a fellow creature. This emblem of death always lies on the judge's desk as he sits, wrapped with his white gloves of purity.

> " Now, by our Lady, Sheriff 'tis hard reckoning,
> That I, with every odds of birth and barony,
> Should be detained here for the casual death
> Of a wild forester, whose utmost having
> Is but the brazen buckle of the belt
> In which he sticks his hedge knife."—*Old Play.*

Staffordshire recently lost a High Sheriff in the person of Colonel Fowler Butler, who completed his final attendance as High Sheriff at the Assizes on the day before his death, the occurrence of which is believed to be unprecedented in the history of this ancient office. The coffin at the funeral was covered with the High Sheriff's purple pall.

The Fowler family, from whom Colonel Fowler Butler traced his descent, were of ancient origin. The first of them known was Richard Fowler, who went on the Crusade with King Richard Cœur de Lion. He was a guard at the King's tent one night, and saved his Majesty's life by intercepting an assassin. For this he was given the " Crest " of the " Vigilant Owl," instead of the " Fowler Snare," and the motto " Garde le Roi." These still form the Fowler crest and motto. The Fowlers have been owners of Pendeford since 1543, when James Fowler inherited the estate from his uncle, Bishop Roland Lee, Henry VIII.'s celebrated minister and President of the Welsh Marshes. Sir Francis Joseph is the present holder of the Shrievalty.

Note.—The Judges wear their Black Caps at the Law Courts on November 9th when they receive the Lord Mayor of London.

HIS WORSHIP THE MAYOR OF STAFFORD.

> " This now remains, right worshipful Sir,
> That carefully you do attend and keep
> The city, wherewithal your sovereign Lord
> Hath put your honour lovingly in trust ;
> That you may add to Stafford's dignity,
> And Stafford's dignity may add to yours."

Remaining in town all that week, I had the pleasure of meeting the Mayor-Elect, who invited me to the Guild Hall on November 9th, Mayor's Day.

The Guild Hall, which I found was opposite the Shire Hall, contained the Council Chamber and Magistrates' Court in one. The Guilds were the forerunners of the Town Councils, and were banished at the Reformation, but the old name still lingers in the buildings were municipal business is conducted, as that other delightful old municipal title, the Mayor's Parlour.

The ceremony of making a new Mayor consists of him being invested with chain and wand, and at the same time a new tablet with the Mayor's name inscribed is added to those of his predecessor on the walls. A flag is hoisted above the building, and the bells of St. Mary's ring out the tidings to the Borough. All the Grammar School boys get a holiday, as the Mayor becomes one of their School Governors, ex-officio.

One of the Mayor's first acts after taking the oath is to appoint certain officials, among whom are his Deputy, his Chaplain, the Ward Aldermen, and Borough Pinner.

An amusing story is preserved as told by the late Sergeant McCabe, an usher of the Crown Court at the Assize, and for many years a police sergeant attached to the Borough Force, concerning the late Borough Pinner named John Perry, whom all can remember in his huge blue watchman's coat and service cap, with red piping round it and the words " Borough Pinner " inscribed thereon.

One night, two young constables, in the course of their beat, found an ass straying about the streets and promptly arrested it. So accordingly they, with their four-footed companion, turned their footsteps in the direction of the official residence of the Borough Pinner in Gaol Road. Arriving at the house, conspicuous with the iron plate over the entrance, denoting the name and function of the occupant, they lifted the latch and walked straight into the kitchen, trailing the ass after them. The household was all a-bed, including old John, who was slightly deaf. The policemen then shouted upstairs :

" John ! John ! Are you there, John ?"

Movements and grunts from up above ; the boards creaked.

" John, we've found a hass up street, but we've pounded him,

Note.—Stafford is one of the oldest boroughs in the country, and in the Council Chamber there was a long list of provosts, bailiffs, and mayors of the borough. From 1164 to 1291 the chief magistrate was called a provost ; from 1291 to 1613 he was called a bailiff ; and from then onwards he was called the Mayor,

John, we've pounded him. Come and see." And so, shortly afterwards, the stairboards creaked as the worthy Pinner clumped down stairs, grumbling all the way, only to find, on reaching the kitchen, that the police had decamped, and confronting him was a braying donkey, who had already broken the sanctuary of John's kitchen by partially chewing up the table cloth left from the previous evening's repast, and in dragging it, had swept the crockery from the table on to the tiled floor with drastic results.

Another notable town official is the Mayor's Sergeant of Mace. This gentleman holds a very ancient office, and attends the Mayor on all official occasions bearing before him that insignia of municipal authority, the Mace.

His picturesque dress consists of velvet knee breeches, gaitors, gilt buttons with the Corporation crest, coat with red cuffs and collar, a white tie, and a glossy silk hat with a band of gold braid round it, completes his attire.

The name sergeant has a very ancient origin, coming from the Latin servire, meaning to serve.

People in early mediæval times often held land by performing a service, and were said to hold their land by Grand Sergeanty.

Lord Stafford held the manor by doing the service of holding the King's stirrup when he came to Stafford.

Ralph de Waymer held the Fish Pond at Stafford on condition that he permitted the King to keep all the pike and bream he could catch when it pleased him to fish there ; while he contented himself by taking as his share " all the other fishes, with the eels, coming to the hooks."

The Earls of Shrewsbury held one seat, Farnham Royal, Buckingham, on condition of fitting the right hand of the King with a glove on the day of his Coronation, and supporting his arm while he held the Sceptre.

Other known instances are feudal lords who for their occupation of certain lands were required to hold the King's head when he crossed the channel and find straw for his bed.

Mr. Justice Talfourd, already mentioned, who died at Stafford, was one of the now obsolete Sergeants at Law. The House of Commons has its Sergeant at Arms, while the Sergeant of the Guard at Buckingham Palace is still termed the " Sergeant in Waiting."

Stafford had, up to recent times, two Sergeants : the Mayor's Sergeant, as well as the Burgesses' Sergeant ; also a Town Crier with bell and staff.

Note.—Baswich Parish Council still appoint a Pinner—the late holder of that office had three cases in forty years.

Note.—In 1717 an Order in Council was made that all Aldermen, and Councillors, were to wear gowns of a dignified character to assist them in maintaining the prestige of their high office. To wear them upon every public fair day and on every Sabbath between Michaelmas and Lady Day. In default to be fined one 1/- for each day, to be levied by the Sergeants.

All these appointments are now merged into one.

Years ago one of the duties of service by the Sergeants was sweeping the Market Place. When the Mayor, with other civic dignatories proceeds in procession round to the Judges' lodging to meet their Lordships, the Mace Bearer is always left at the door with the Mace, so that the Mayor's emblem of power shall not be flaunted before the King's Judges.

The Mace is now of gold. But when the Mace had sterner uses it was made of harder material. Milton speaks of Death's "mace petrific," Chaucer of a 'mace of stele," and it was with one of iron that Walworth laid low Wat Tyler. Iron maces, too, were used by the Turks in their wars of the dark ages. When the mace passed from being a weapon of war to a mere emblem of authority its intrinsic value was increased, for it was made first of copper, then of silver, often richly gilt, and now of the most precious metal.

In the year A.D. 1354 the City of London received privileges of having their maces and swords carried upright. All other Corporations slope their swords and maces on ceremonial occasions, with the exception of Stafford, whose Mace Bearer bears it upright. London's privilege was at one time contested by the City of York who claimed to have an equal sovereign right with London to bear its swords and maces in the same manner as the City of London, but in 1873 the question was fully considered and the Corporation of York relinquished its claim. It is curious that Stafford should share this unique privilege.

Note.—The ceremony of Mayor making differs in many towns from the custom at Stafford. At Dunstable, for instance, the Mayor is subjected to the time honoured, but disagreeable, ceremony of "bumping." At Bournemouth, always decorous, the Mayor is kissed by the retiring Mayor. The Mayor of Lincoln is inducted by having placed on his finger an ancient ring worn by hundreds of his predecessors in office. Grantham taps its new Mayor on the head with the Town Clerk's mallet !

LORD HIGH STEWARD AND THE LORD OF THE MANOR.

" Look, who that is most virtuous always,
Privee and apert,* and most entendeth aye,
To do the gentle deedes that he can,
And take him for the greatest gentleman."—*Chaucer.*

Among the officials that are appointed by the Town Council are two gentlemen whose appointments have been made by that body since early times, and the first is the People's Warden of St. Mary's Church, and the second is the Lord High Steward of the Borough. The former is elected at a meeting of the Town Council on St. Thomas' Day, when they exercise this important privilege once a year.

*Secretly and openly.

The latter appointment is made at the death of a **High Steward,** and when a new Steward is made the office extends over the life of the recipient. The Lord High Steward elect is summoned to a meeting of the Town Council and attends at the Council Chamber for the ceremony of initiation.

The Steward is presented with a wand and ring, which become the property of the Steward and usually devolve as heirlooms in his family.

The duties of Lord High Steward are to attend at all Royal visits to Stafford and perform the introduction of the Mayor and Corporation to the visiting Royalty, and then remain in attendance. He is also required to intercede with the King on behalf of the town authorities, when called upon, should the occasion arise. The office is, in common with all others connected with this ancient town, one of great antiquity.

In 1455 it is known to be held by Humphrey Stafford, Duke of Buckingham, the famous ancestor of the present holder of the office, Baron Stafford. This Humphrey exercised his office by arbitration in settling some disputes between the Prior of St. Thomas' (the priory with the lady spectre) and the town in this case. It concerned the lordship of Coton, part of which is in cultivation by the burgesses of Stafford to this day. The lordship of Coton is held by the present Lord Stafford, in return for which he must hold the King's stirrup when he visits Stafford.

Another famous holder of the office was James, Duke of Monmouth, in 1676, who raised a rebellion and was crushed at the battle of Sedgemoor by the forces of James II.

I wonder what the feelings of Staffordians were to their Steward. Instead of pleading for the burgesses, he had to plead for his life, but his head was cut off nevertheless. He probably owed this office to Sir Thomas Armstrong, member of parliament for Stafford, who became one of his fellow conspirators about a year after this appointment. Armstrong, who was executed for his share in the Monmouth Rebellion, gave £40 to be divided between eight burgesses, to be used for two years free of interest.

Note.—After the execution a portion of Armstrong's remains were sent to Stafford and set up as a warning.

" All that's now left of him is a skeleton grim,
  The stoutest to strike with dismay,
So ghastly the sight, that no urchin at night,
  Who can help it will pass by that way.
Chains round his middle, and chains round his neck,
  A banquet for crows on his carcase to batten ;
And the unctuous morsels that fell from their feast
  Served the rank weeds beneath him to fatten."

The earliest known Sheriff was a Lord Stafford, appointed in 1087, the last year of William the Conqueror's reign.

STAFFORD CASTLE.

In 1485 Stafford Castle was the scene of a meeting the outcome of which was of great importance in the history of England. The Duke of Richmond, as Henry VII. then was, arrived at Stafford with his army on the way to Bosworth Field. Here he had a secret interview with Sir William Stanley, the result of which was seen at the Battle of Bosworth when the Stanleys changed sides.

Proceeding on to Tamworth tradition has it that Henry lagged behind his escort and got lost purposely to keep a secret rendezvous with the Stanleys at their home near by, Haselour Hall. This is, however, very unlikely, as the scheme needed more secrecy than straggling off like a deserter to a house possibly full of spies.

Shakespeare makes him mention the conference with the Stanleys in his play " Richard the Third ":

" Fellows in arms, and my most loving friends,
Bruised beneath the yoke of tyranny,
Thus far into the bowels of the land
Have we marched on without impediment,
And here receive we from our father Stanley
Lines of fair comfort and encouragement.
The wretched bloody and usurping boar,
That soiled your summerfields and fruitful vines,
Swills your warm blood like wash and makes his trough
In your embowelled bosoms, this foul swine
Lies even now in the centre of this isle ;
Near to the town of Leicester, as we learn,
From Tamworth hither is but one day's march,
In God's name cheerly on, courageous friends,
To reap the harvest of perpetual piece
By this one bloody trial of sharp war.

Queen Elizabeth was loyally entertained at Stafford Castle when, after a sojourn at Chartley Castle, she continued her progress to Stafford, and after the civic reception, proceeded down Crowberi Lane (Crabbery Street) and was supposed to have refreshed herself at the Noah's Ark Inn. (The fame of its ale must have been known even then). Crossing the river at Broad Eye the cavalcade continued to the Castle.

Her retinue was so enormous that the Castle's accommodation was insufficient to house " all the Queen's horses and all the Queen's men," and so tents were pitched in the fields around and the horses tethered ; the whole assuming the appearance of an enormous pleasure fair.

The Castle witnessed stern days during the Civil War, when, after being mysteriously evacuated by Lady Stafford and its Royalist defenders, was governed by a Captain Stone for the Parliament, and was later pulled down by Sir W. Brereton, with the exception of a few walls.

During these wars a Vernon Yonge, was executed in front of it. Among the ancient features still to be seen is the original moat, now dry, which encircles the present structure, the remains of a huge shield bearing the town arms, the original well, and the glorious view from the battlements.

The wood that surrounds it has been particularly rich in finds of the Castle's stormy past. Some cannon balls, a plain silver cross, and a lobster Cromwellian helmet, still to be seen at Haughton, the lower portion of a large font, silver coins of Edward VI., being found, among other things.

The present owner, whose residence is at Swynnerton Hall, has a wonderful view of the Castle of his forbears.

It will be noticed that the church at the foot of the castle contains no tombs of the early Staffords ; this occurs through the Staffords having a religious foundation of their own at Stone, and their interments were made there, where prayers were said for the repose of their souls. Some later Staffords were buried in Castle Church.

The old abbey church of Stone was full of the magnificent monuments of the great baronial family of Stafford. These monuments blazed in gold and heraldic colour, and over them doubtless hung the battle-stained shields of the mighty dead.

Swynnerton Hall stands out on a spur of the hill, and from the terrace the line of the horizon shows Stafford Castle set out boldly in its belt of trees, proudly dominating the countryside, which, no doubt, is a very pleasant view to the present Baron.

His Old Masters are the admiration of visitors, and on occasions he pilots some learned society round and points out those of his various ancestors, many of whom lost their heads on the block.

One great picture portrays James II. and his children ; being shown to the Old Stafford Society one day, a member pointed to the little boy and asked if he was the Old Pretender. The feeling of ancestry was too much for the kind host (the late Baron), whose forebears had suffered exile with that monarch, and whose children had played and been brought up with those little children in the big picture. Quite kindly he said :

" You may call him the Pretender, but we call him the King."

So after all these years there were still followers of the White Cockade, faithful in spirit to the lost Stewart cause.

Which reminds one of our National Anthem, for as originally written the words, " long to reign over us," read, " soon to reign over us," and meant " send him soon across the water back to the throne of England." The first verse of the National Anthem in its original form reads :   God save our Native King,
God save the King !
Send him victorious,
Happy and glorious,
Soon to reign over us,
God save the King !

Among all changes and alterations since, the significant word " send " in the third line remains as evidence of its Jacobite origin.

Note.—In the days of the exiled Charles II., when to drink his health in water was the sign that one was hoping for his return from across the Channel. An echo of this is to be found when one dines with the Scots Guards. Being suspected of disloyalty to the Cromwellians, the officers were not allowed to use finger bowls in case they secretly drank Charles' health while holding their wine over the bowls. To this day you will see no finger bowls in the officers' mess.

MAYOR SUNDAY.

Sunday saw me in glossy silk hat making my way through lines of soldiery into the Borough Hall to pay my respects to His Worship, who, with the Town Clerk, was standing either side of a small table laden with the Town Mace and the two seals. All these originally were carried in front of the Mayor on State occasions, but now only the large Mace is borne aloft. It is designed to unscrew, so that it forms a beautiful loving cup at the Corporation banquets.

I was greeted by several I knew in the hall, and heard one man complaining of the cold and wishing again for the days when mulled wine was served to the company on Mayor's Sunday.

The entry of the Borough Member, a Cabinet Minister, caused a general stir. Although I did not know him, his great Imperial work was well-known to me ; a man esteemed by all parties, which says much for him ; a man living for the Empire and willing to serve all parties in furtherance of the greatness of our Empire.

The crashing of drums outside announced the starting of the procession, and I found myself paired off with another by a dexterous superintendent of police, who sorted out the sheep from the goats by sending the County Magistrates, Councillors, etc., first, and visitors last.

As we got outside the sun broke through the fog and glimmered on the firemen's helmets in front. Down Eastgate Street wound the long procession into Tipping Street, which, my half-section informed me, was named after Sheridan's election bribes which took place here. Into Greengate we turned, crossed the river Sowe into Bridge Street, turning right by the Library.

" Good collection in there," my informative friend remarked. " Wragge Museum, only no room to show half ! Stafford has some wonderful treasures all hidden away out of sight, Sir."

We were now passing the King Edward VI. Grammar School, and my friend, after scanning the long lines of building, said, " You didn't know ' Jacky,' I suppose ? " I assented. " Splendid fellow, chapel every morning, and we had a fine service, everyone enjoyed

Note.—Mayors and Corporations are the butt of many jests, few realising their great service. The following is typical :—Ian Hay, to a pupil " Walpole, the best thing that you can hope for is that one day, with luck, you may become Mayor of a very small town."

it except the boys who had to stand at the Lectern and read the Lessons." My friend seemed rather saddened by these recollections, but I was eager to learn more.

" The boys have a holiday every Mayor's Day, I understand ?"

" Why, yes," he replied, " but I was telling you about the service we used to have in the old chapel. At the end of every term we had a special service and prayers for the boys who were leaving, and tears welled up in the Head's eyes. How we sang the favourite hymn, ' Truly Blessed is the Station,' and Billy Lambert, who played the organ, always wondered why we sang this hymn so fervently."

I was about to ask when he broke out again.

" But it was Empire Day that the Head always thought so much of, and the whole school was assembled, the cadets paraded, and with these at the head the school marched through the field and down the drive to the school house door, where the Head, mortar-board in hand, would stand opposite our proudly waving flag where we could salute it and then march on into chapel, to be regaled with an address on citizenship and the meaning of Empire Day. He was a great man for the Empire."

We were now nearing the pealing bells of St. Mary's, and passed through the double lines of Yeomanry, Artillery, Ambulance, Girl Guides, Boy Scouts, and a host of others, into the Church, where we were accommodated with seats high up the Church in a place of honour.

A troop of Yeomanry, with swords and jangling spurs, followed up, and were all seated in the chancel together. " Staffordshire Yeomanry," whispered my friend, who saw me glancing that way. " Very old county regiment ; head the procession," he whispered. They had taken off their large cavalry swords, which would incommode them in kneeling, and had passed them along to one at the end, who ranged them round a pillar near the pulpit.

From where I sat the Aston Tombs in the North Transept, with the faded banners above, swaying slightly with the draught, could be seen. Then the Rector mounted the pulpit in his Chaplain's robes, and announced his text, " Ye shall turn your swords into plough-shares and your spears into pruning hooks." I wondered to myself how astonished those proud Yeomen would be if, instead of the swords facing the preacher, there were ploughshares instead.

The conclusion of the service came all too quickly, and after the procession had reformed, and again reached the Borough Hall, I bade farewell of His Worship and my new friend, and returned to the Swan.

As I entered the Swan, the barrister, who was still here, asked me if I would like to join the Stafford Troop of Yeomanry, in which he was an officer, in their annual lunch, held by custom on Mayor's Sunday. I readily consented, and, during the lunch, received from one of them a copy of their history which, later on, in the train, I commenced to read.

THE STAFFORDSHIRE YEOMANRY.

The Queen's Own Royal Regiment of Staffordshire Yeomanry, whose regimental headquarters are situated at the Barracks in Bailey Street, Stafford, was formed in this town in the year 1794.

This year saw the forming of Yeomanry Corps in many counties in aid of the civil power, for the preservation of the public peace. In that capacity the Regiment has always assisted with the utmost forbearance in discharge of their sometimes painful duties, but they have no " Peterloo " to regret, and were said never to have drawn their swords without necessity, nor even sheathed without honour, a sentiment in which all Staffordians will readily concur. The regiment has seen much service, both civil and military, during which they have witnessed some curious things and been present at some thrilling escapades.

In the 138 years of official life, their incidents have included such as coal strikes, the recovery of John o' Gaunt's treasure chests, the stampede at Bishops Stortford, entry into Jericho, Jordon Valley, bread riots at Stafford, besides incidents in South Africa at the birth of the 20th century.

What a thrilling list, what scenes to conjure up before the imagination. The gorgeous reviews on Whittington Heath, when the mounted band, in white and silver, would lead the Regiment with sparkling equipment and headed by their colours and guidons, past King Edward and the assembled company.

Owing to the troublesome state of the times, immediately upon Parliament giving permission for Volunteer Cavalry forces to be raised, a committee composed of the deputy-lieutenants and magistrates was formed in Staffordshire, and started a fund. Subscriptions were received for the purpose of arming and clothing. A meeting of county magnates was convened by Earl Gower at Stafford, and from it a committee was formed. This was on 4th July, 1794, when the Articles of Enrolment were drawn up by the committee, and they then met once a fortnight and continued to do so for some time after the regiment was formed. The Articles also stated that the members of the Regiment were enrolled for the internal defence and security of the Kingdom during the present war, on the following conditions :

" To receive no pay, unless when embodied or called out, but to attend, mounted on a serviceable horse, not less than fourteen hands and a half high, for the purpose of exercise. The horse to be approved by the Commanding Officer of each troop. When so assembled to receive pay as cavalry, and to be subject to military discipline. Each person attending on the day of exercise to wear a uniform at the expense of the county subscriptions, together with arms and accoutrements provided by the Government. Each troop to consist of not less than fifty men, officers included. The pay received from the

Government by any persons enrolled, as well as by commissioned officers, as others, to be equally divided amongst the corps.''

The uniform of the corps was a short scarlet coatee, turned back at the bottom with yellow cloth, and the same coloured collars and cuffs. The silver buttons were placed in twos down the front, like a Lord Lieutenant's state dress. The breeches were of white leather with military knee boots. A bear-skin hat with feather and the Hanoverian black cockade, white gloves, belts and waistcoats completed this gorgeous attire, the officers being distinguished by a crimson sash worn over the waistcoat. This is not all, however, the military gentlemen of the county were required to have their hair dressed and queued.

The horse furniture comprised a white head stall, harness of brown leather, the saddle being covered with a bright blue saddle-cloth with a double white border and a white rose in the rear corner (later the rose was succeeded by the regimental badge), white cloak cases edged with red, and pistol holsters covered with bearskin flounces.

Their arms were pistols and old fashioned swords with black leather hilts and scabbards. The swords might easily have belonged to Cromwell's ironsides, by the look of them, for they were entirely devoid of ornament, being very plain, strong, and workmanlike, and one could easily imagine them as part of the equipment of the New Model Army. After the Civil Wars and the Protectorate had passed on, and the standing army was reduced, it is possible that these swords were stored in the Tower of London with other equipment, to lie there until an economic government would use them up on county formations This may be the history of those fine-tempered raking weapons of offence.

The inaugural meeting of the Regiment took place at Stafford on the 8th August, the same year as the Badge and Motto were adopted. The former was the badge of the followers of Lord Stafford, and the latter '' Pro aris et focis,'' and a very fine motto too. ('' For hearth and home.'').

The names of the first five troops raised were the
Newcastle Troop, raised by Col. Earl Gower.
Stafford Troop, raised by Lt.-Col. Hon. E. Monckton.
Lichfield Troop, raised by Major E. P. Elliot.
Leek Troop, raised by Capt. J. Bulkeley.
Walsall Troop, raised by Capt. W. Tennant.
Which makes a total of 250 all ranks when first enrolled, probably other supernumeraries would make a roll of 300 men.

Officers attended all parts of the county for the purposes of enlistments. The original officers' commissions are preserved in the archives of the Regimental Headquarters, signed by the King, as was then the custom, in the top left-hand corner. In those days age was no bar to holding a commission, some were officers at the early age of 16 or 17.

The force was, from the first, warmly welcomed by the county in general, which gave security to altars and homes, and the utmost enthusiasm prevailed among the members of the Regiment. Drills were proposed for two mornings in the week, for two or three hours duration.

An entry in Alrewas Church Register states the Regiment during 1794 " were trained and disciplined on Fradley Heath," where the point-to-point races are now held.

The committee responsible continued to meet at Stafford.

Some of the officers commissions were dated September 20th, 1795, including the Colonel's, whose original commission is still extant.

The Yeomanry were liable to be called out at any moment, ready to march to any part of the Kingdom should the country be invaded. The order would come either from the King, or his representatives in the county, the Lord Lieutenant, or the High Sheriff.

Members were fined for being absent from parades, and in the records appears a fine of 2s. 6d. in case any member should fire off his pistol or use his arms or accoutrements in the field or else-where without an order, or in a wanton, unsoldierly-like manner.

There was an attempted riot at Radford Bridge on August 8th.

Next month, the 21st October, 1795, three divisions of troops were paraded in Stafford, being mustered for exercise. Two days later these troops, under the Colonel, Lord Gower, for the purpose of receiving colours, were formed up in Stafford Market Place, forming three sides of a square. Lieut.-Col. Monckton placed himself near the window of the Star Inn, accompanied by the Cornets of the three troops. Lord Gower's wife, the Countess of Sutherland, then handed the standards through the window to the Colonel, whom she addressed as follows :

" I am very happy to have the honour to deliver these standards to this very loyal and constitutional regiment ; two are from myself, and the third I am commissioned to present by the Marchioness of Donegal, who is prevented from delivery in person. We have no doubt that they will be well defended by the known loyalty, spirit and courage of the gentlemen of the County of Stafford."

Lieut.-Col. Monckton made a suitable reply, and the standards were consecrated by the Chaplain.

Colonel Lord Gower Sutherland (as he was then addressed) then rode into the centre of the square, and addressed the three divisions of the Regiment :

" Gentlemen,—I feel extreme satisfaction in seeing here assembled so well-appointed and so well disciplined a regiment. When we enrolled ourselves last year in defence of our property, and in support of our King and Country in case of invasion, I had great hopes that we should prove ourselves of utility to our country. My hopes have been fully realised. During the course of the summer, you, gentlemen, have shown your alacrity and courage in preventing disturbances in different parts of the country. Your county now looks upon you with gratitude for past services and with confidence in your future exertions.''

The ceremony was concluded by cheers, no doubt heartily subscribed to by the assembled townsfolk, and the masons busy on the new Shire Hall. This is why the ceremony of presenting the colours had to be carried out through the medium of the window of the Star Inn.

The Yeomanry then marched to the field where it was exercised for some time and acquitted itself in such a manner as to merit the entire satisfaction of all present.

On 4th June, 1796, it is recorded that the Stafford Troop paraded in honour of King George III's birthday. The next year saw the great victory of Sir John Jervis, who, at the Battle of St. Vincent, destroyed the Spanish Fleet, and Colonel Earl Gower, at a levee three months later, alluded to this occasion, when he presented a petition to His Majesty assuring him of the loyalty and affection of the armed Yeomanry of Stafford, during the present critical time of war without and intestine disturbances within the country.

1798 records the arrest of several persons in Manchester for high treason, who, being sent to London, were escorted by part of the Yeomanry through Staffordshire.

Unrest so increased this year, coupled by great fears of invasion by Napolean, that additional forces were raised, under the Additional Forces Act, called Armed Associations, consisting of three companies of Infantry and a troop of Volunteer Cavalry, for use in defending the county, should the Yeomanry be ordered to other parts of the country, or to meet the enemy in case of invasion. Five of these association troops were raised :

Royal Pottery, or Stanley Troop, commanded by Capt. Josiah Spode.
The Loyal Bilston Troop.
The Tamworth Troop.
The Wolverhampton Troop.

These four troops were eventually drafted into the county Regiment of Staffordshire Yeomanry.

A Handsworth Troop, raised by the loyal Handsworth Association, was independent of the county regiment for the whole of its thirty years' existence.

Two more local troops were raised, the Stone and Eccleshall Troop, whose dress differed by wearing scarlet-faced coatees with black and gold lace.

Adjutants were now allowed to Yeomanry Regiments, the drill sergeant appears, and a permanent trumpeter to each troop, the total strength of volunteer forces, including independent troops totalled 600.

The services of the regiment were deemed valuable enough for the Government to pay for the whole of the arms and clothing, and remitted to it £2,412.

A.D. 1800 saw the retirement of the founder of the Regiment, being succeeded by Colonel Monckton, whose troop (the Stafford Troop) was called out twice in September, at Stafford, under Lieut. Keen, to quell riots there owing to the high prices of provisions, a regular force of Dragoons assisting them in putting down this riot. One of the occasions showed signs of an ugly situation, as fire arms were used by the mob, which wounded several people.

The riots spread, however, to the Potteries and continued a whole week there, the mob having raided the provision shops and sold the food at ridiculous prices.

The Newcastle troop, and more Dragoons, stationed at Lane End, were repeatedly called out to preserve order. Wolverhampton also saw four days rioting, the Lichfield and Walsall Troops being publicly thanked by the Mayor for their prompt assistance.

One can imagine the relief householders would feel (the mob hammered on their shutters for admission) after the word fled round like magic that the Yeomanry had been sent for.

1800 also saw a Troop raised by Lord Bradford at Weston-under-Lizard, and known as the Weston Troop, the Regiment being now three squadrons strong.

Peace was made with France in 1802, but all troops, except Walsall, volunteered to remain enrolled as their assistance might still be necessary to aid the local civil powers. The infantry bodies of the Armed Associations were however, disbanded.

1803 saw War again declared with Napoleon and fears of imminent invasion. A meeting was held at Stafford and it was agreed that the Regiment be augmented. An independent Troop was raised at Uttoxeter by Claude Bagot.

Mr. Littleton also raised a Troop of men living at Penkridge, Wyrley, Cannock and other hamlets near, making the regiment total 487. A Batchacre Troop totalling 40 is mentioned in the Army list, but this troop only existed six years, and very little appears to have been known about it.

In 1804 Col. Delves Broughton of Broughton, inspected the entire regiment at Stafford during its eight days training, commencing Sunday as usual ; it would be interesting to know where the Yeomanry manœuvred at Stafford. Col. Broughton was highly pleased with the discipline " that although there were nearly 500 men quartered in the town, the utmost order and regularity had been observed."

Now appear carbines as weapons of regimental offence, they being issued 12 to each troop, which were carried by men on the flanks of squadrons, who acted as skirmishers. The weekly parades of each troop continued, except in time of harvest, and as the power of France and Spain had been broken at the Battle of Trafalgar, there was no further anxiety of invasion.

The Volunteer Infantry at Stafford attended St. Mary's, when a sermon was preached by the Rector, the text being : " Rejoice with Trembling." This was Thanksgiving Day, 5th December, 1805. Next month the great bell of St. Mary's was tolled once a minute during the time of Nelson's interment in the Crypt of St. Paul's Cathedral.

So enthusiasm, alarms, and fears of war subsided and faded, and several troops ceased to exist, but in 1808, a mounted band was added to the Regiment, and filled a great need. These were raised and equipped at the expense of the officers and were clothed in white jackets with blue braid. The drum banners are still preserved at the Bailey Street Barracks. The regimental uniform also underwent a change at this time, and in the same barracks is a very interesting picture, showing the various changes that the uniform has undergone.

1810 brings another riot at Wolverhampton on market day, 30th May, when it commenced by the mob throwing the butchers' meat from the stalls into the streets, overturning them, wrenching off the tilts, causing a great crowd to collect, with so much free meat going begging. The promotors of the riot tried to get a regiment of local militia on to their side, but in this attempt, through the firmness of the Colonel and officers, they were entirely unsuccessful, and, with the exception of a few, who deserted to the other side, the militia remained steady and the riot crushed.

One wonders how the poor market people fared over their wrecked joints and damaged food.

The next day saw the arrival of the Teddesley and Weston Troops, and, with the rioting subsiding, troops seized the ringleaders and they were committed to jail.

A letter in 1810 sent by an inspecting officer to the C.O. complains of the slackness shown on parade by the Bilston and Walsall Troops, noting that they did not arrive on the parade ground till half an hour later than the time fixed, and, what few of the Bilston Troop attended came scampering on the ground as if they were coming to a meet—a pack of foxhounds—rather than a military parade, and also complains of the drill sergeant in giving to a recruit a pistol, quite useless from neglect, and his own not much better.

Five years later sees the Lichfield Troop welcoming the gallant Marquis of Anglesey on his return from the wars, having lost a leg at Waterloo, where he was in command of the allied cavalry. The Yeomen took the horses out of the traces and pulled the carriage to the Guild Hall at Lichfield.

Later, in November, the Prince Regent paid a visit to the Marquis at Beaudesert, posted up from London for that purpose. The Royal party arrived at Lichfield attended by a travelling escort of Yeomanry, going to the George Inn, the streets being lit up by hundreds of blazing torches. Here the Marquis' horses awaited them, but the postillions had been ordered to take the Prince to Beaudesert Park and had to be forcibly restrained from going thither. One can imagine the crowd outside the George, the wrangling and shouting round the coach, the Princes, for one of his brothers was with him, looking out with amazement on the noisy scene ; horses frightened by the blazing torches that lit up the street, rearing and plunging as they were taken out of the traces, and the Marquis' horses backed in. The mud-stained white breeches of the Yeomanry escort, with faces blackened by the smoke from the torches, trying to keep order and generally expedite the departure with dignity.

Their troubles were not over, however, for as the carriage containing the bowing Princes was driven away to the cheers of the gathered populace, the horses, going down a hill some distance out of Lichfield, became restive, and owing to the darkness and the fact that in the excitement someone had omitted to light the carriage lamps, the whole concern was run into a ditch. No one being hurt, the carriage was righted and proceeded further without mishap. There is no record of the feelings of the two Princes on this occasion, who were quarrelled over like a bone and then thrown into a ditch on a pitch black night in November, and they are not to be imagined. The Prince Regent had apparently recovered sufficiently next morning to address a letter to the Colonel of the Regiment, expressing his appreciation of the attention paid by the Yeomanry on his arrival, and regret at not arriving in time to see the Corps—and privately, also the road to Beaudesert, as then the Princes might not have been overturned.

Civil disturbances continued in different parts of the county, owing to lowering of wages and lack of employment.

The march of the Blanketeers, the meeting of the Radicals at Manchester, riots in the mining districts, Parliamentary elections, presentation dinners in the Shire Hall, Stafford, Salutes on the King's birthday, great riots at Derby, etc.; all these events made the duties, which were carried out in a thorough forebearing and admirable way by the Staffordshire Yeomanry.

I looked up with a start, to see that my train had reached its destination, and, putting away the rest of the history, jammed on my hat and hurried away.

Later the " midnight oil " burned in my room as I again picked up this book, arranged the pillows and thrilled, as the words " Treasure Chest " caught my eye.

THE LOST TREASURE CHEST.

" Fifteen men on a dead man's chest."—*R.L.S.*

The jealousies of the various political parties of Plantagenet days, which seems a far cry from 1831, led to scenes of minor battles, scenes of bloodshed and other disturbances.

Tutbury Castle was then the princely residence of Thomas, Earl of Lancaster, nephew of Edward I., and cousin of the new King, Edward II. This Earl of Lancaster was at the head of a strong party of English nobles, who were opposed to the weak Edward's favourites, who, gaining many privileges and favours from the new King, naturally invited the envy of many, particularly as they were foreign, and first amongst them was Piers de Gaveston.

Troubles followed in the wake of the arrogant Gaveston, who was eventually executed by the indirect influence of the Earl of Lancaster in 1312. King Edward soon filled his place by more foreigners, the Despencers, and the Earl's hatred was now focussed on them, which was no small thing, as for the last few years succeeding the Battle of Bannockburn, he had practically ruled England in all but name.

The weak spirit of the King was at last stirred, and he suddenly surprised the Earl by enrolling an army at Coventry, perhaps on the pretext of gathering a hunting party, and hastened to Burton-on-Trent, where the Earl was busily trying to prevent a force of the King's soldiers from crossing the river. He was assisted by augmented forces under the Earl of Hereford, who was allied to him against the foreign foe. The Royal army arriving near Burton, their van guard was repulsed at the river bridge—a very narrow and crooked bridge, with angles and projections and with chapels and other buildings, made its defence easy and the crossing doubtful.

While this was taking place the rear portion of the Royal army was detached and sent along the river where they were able to cross near Walton, and surprised the rebels in the rear. Panic ensued following on this shock, and the Earl, hastily gathering his valuables and treasure chest from Tutbury Castle, while his followers set fire to the village, then decamped, crossing the river Dove in such a hurry on their way up to Pontefract Castle, to which impenetratable stronghold the two Earls decided to retreat, that the treasure chest was lost in traversing the river, and sank into its swift flowing stream and mud, which was very often in flood. The current being very strong, the wagon horses conveying the baggage, in charge of Leicester, the treasurer, would probably be swept off their feet and the contents upset, danger of pursuit precluding its recovery at the time.

At the Battle of Boroughbridge, the two Earls were defeated, the Earl of Hereford being slain, and the Earl of Lancaster was taken prisoner and brought back to Pontefract Castle, where, after imprisonment there, he was executed by the King's orders.

The question of the treasure chest then occupied the attention of the King, who sent his Justices in Eyre to inquire concerning it, and other forfeited goods and chattels of the late Earl. The Abbot of Burton came under suspicion and was charged at that Assize in 1324 '' with being illegally in possession of £400 pounds worth of the effects.''

This was denied by the Lord Abbot, but an adverse jury found a verdict against him of £300. The Abbot appealed to the King, who was hunting in Needwood Forest, and, maintaining his innocence, obtained a promise of pardon. The Judgment, however, had been forwarded to London, and a commission writ was issued for the amount and sent to Burton Abbey to levy the fine. The Abbot again appealed to the King, who announced a day in London when he would make a decision on the merits of the case. On the day appointed the Abbot was successful in having the judgement squashed. The whole of the correspondence and evidence was recorded in the Chartulory of Burton Abbey, written in French. His innocence could have been further established, for, at that very time, the treasure chest still lay under the ooze of the bed of the River Dove.

On the glorious 1st of June, 1831, on clearing the mill race of that river, where sheep sometimes drown, a number of silver coins were found sixty yards below the bridge.

The proprietor of the Cotton Mills at Tutbury, wishing to increase his water power, commenced operations, which resulted in this find. They were about half a yard below the surface of the gravel, as if they had been washed from a higher course. The men naturally left their work and commenced the more profitable task of "gold digging." Silver coins were discovered by the thousand. As they advanced up the river the more successful they became, and on the 8th June, they discovered the main deposit.

Never was such a treasure hunt. Silver was thrown on the bank by the shovel-full ; nearly 5,000 coins were collected by two men in one day, who sold them to the bystanders at 6s. to 8s. 6d. per 100.

This main deposit was about three yards square near the Derbyshire side of the river.

A large crowd collected as news of the treasure spread rapidly all over the country-side, and the scene became the site of a miniature "gold rush !" Quarrels and fights became frequent, and things became so ugly that the local magistrates appealed for a force of Yeomanry. The Burton Troop of Staffordshire Yeomanry, under Lieutenant Peel, soon rode to the scene, preserved order, and guarded the treasure.

The total number of coins ultimately counted was 100,000, all silver, dated during the reign of Henry III., Edward I., and Edward II., with a few Scotch and foreign coins. Part of those first found were claimed by the Duchy of Lancaster, and are now to be seen in the British Museum. The Yeomanry remained on duty two days, when they were relieved by regulars, but remained under arms at Burton for another day, no doubt as a precautionary measure.

Further searches were made on behalf of the Crown until July 1st, when another 1,500 coins were despatched to London. A final search was made in 1883.

There are still a few coins treasured in the neighbourhood.

Note.—The Scotch coin was for paying Scotch levies in Lancaster's intended Rebellion to wrest the Throne of England from King Edward.

The authorities then had that portion of the bed of the river gravelled over to prevent any further search.

Thus the Staffordshire Yeomanry figured in that romantic hunt for the Earl of Lancaster's treasure, and shows how monks, rioters, feudal lords, princes, kings, and yeomen were mixed up in the various scenes connected with the losing and finding of a treasure, bridging an interval of five centuries.

The Yeomanry continued to perform its work of service to all, riots were quelled, and they were even used to protect property during fires—what a boon to the County these Yeomen were.

Eighteen thirty-nine saw the Chartist Riots in Birmingham, when terrible damage was done and lives lost. Eighteen forty-three saw more peaceful duties discharged, such as escorting Queen Victoria, who came on a visit to the County. Eighteen forty-five saw the presentation to the Regiment of twelve silver trumpets, presented by the ladies of the county, and still in use on state occasions ; the old flint-lock pistols replaced by carbines ; and the annual duty was performed at Lichfield, which for some time past had been the regimental head-quarters, Yeomanry House being the permanent address of the regiment.

THE YEOMANRY BALLS.

"And thrash the cad who says you waltz too well."—*Kipling*.

The Yeomanry Balls, which are, and were, famed for their brilliance and excellence, are so important a function that some mention of them seems necessary.

On January 10th, 1895, the Stafford Troop gave a ball at the Borough Hall, Stafford. The programme, one of which is still extant, bears on the front "Queen's Own Royal Regiment Staffordshire Yeomanry," and shows a lady in military uniform, possibly the Queen, field glasses in hand, gazing from an eminence over an expanse of country. She is adorned by a red coat with braided cuffs, with a tiny waist, wearing a green skirt with red piping bordering it, and a crest in one corner, whilst a yellow sash streams from the left side. A pill-box hat and a riding whip complete the startling effect.

In Stafford House, now known as the London Museum, which is next door to St. James' Palace, there is a collection of similar uniforms to these, worn by Queen Victoria when reviewing her troops.

A list of dances, of which there are twenty-three, with the music, are on the other side of the programme. The dances were always announced by the Regimental Quartermaster, who came into the ballroom bearing a lance with pennon (the Yeomanry colours) attached. He proceeded to claim attention by tapping the butt end on the floor, and then to announce the next dance with great dignity.

1. Polka .... " En Chasse."
2. Valse .... " Carlotta."
3. Lancers .... " Songs of London."
4. Valse .... " Whisper and I shall hear."
5. Barn Dance .... " Charmian."
6. Valse .... " Royal Betrothal."
7. Lancers .... " Utopia."
8. Valse .... " La Serenata."
9. Polka .... " Ting-a-Ling."
10. Barn Dance .... " Popcorn."

Supper Dances.
1. Valse .... " Cloister."
2. Schott .... " Coringa."
3. Valse .... " Venus Reigen."

11. Valse .... " Santiago."
12. Lancers .... " Oh, Mr. Porter."
13. Valse .... " Loves Old Sweet Song."
14. Quadrille .... " La Cigale."
15. Valse .... " Love's Dream."
16. Barn Dance .... " Iola."
17. Polka .... " Ring o' Bells."
18. Lancers .... " Round the Town."
19. Schott .... " Balmoral."
20. Valse .... " Acclamations."
    Gallop .... " John Peel."

The Yeomanry always took the rowels out of their spurs at the Yeomanry Ball.

A curious half-gallon jug in the possession of the Old Stafford Society was apparently made to commemorate the enlistment in the Yeomanry of William Southern, whose picture in the original uniform, mounted, is portrayed on the side of the jug, and states that William Southern joined the Q.O.R.B. Staffs. Yeomanry Cavalry, 2nd February, 1802. This jug was presented by his descendants 127 years later on the occasion of the Old Stafford exhibition in the Stafford Free Library, when, by special permission of the Adjutant, many of the regimental relics of the Yeomanry were shown altogether for the first time.

In this exhibition were also several Yeomanry medals, one of them being the Imperial Medal, with white ribbon, for South Africa, whilst another was struck about 1843, and presented to those on duty at Shugborough Hall, for guarding visiting Royalty there.

A khaki covered prayer book is preserved amongst the regimental trophies. It was used by the Chaplain during the South African War. On the fly-leaf is written " Lord, into Thy hands I commit my body."

They even had their annual training during 1865, when, owing to the serious cattle plague, the Government had written that they might dispense with the annual duty ; but the Staffordshire Yeomanry turned out as usual, and were one of the few Yeomanry Regiments that did so that year. Riots had now almost expired, but in 1867, the Wolverhampton Troop, under Captain Perry, was called out on February 22nd on account of an anticipated riot in the town during the visit of a man named Murphy, who was lecturing against Popery.

Disturbances had followed in the wake of this nuisance, and, so perturbed were the magistrates, that a troop of Hussars were also sent for. The town was patrolled until late at night when all became quiet. This was the only occasion that the Yeomanry figured in religious matters, but it was all one and the same to them when duty called.

Eighteen seventy-two saw Mr. Gladman as bandmaster, and he arranged the regimental march, called St. Patrick's Day, from a tune presented to the regiment by a former Duchess of York, there being about eighteen bandsmen at this time.

The annual duty at Lichfield in 1894, the Centenary of the Regiment was celebrated, the Commander being the Duke of Sutherland, whose ancestor raised the Corps a hundred years ago. In the regimental archives is still the beautifully illuminated address presented to the Duke by the Mayor and Corporation of Lichfield on that occasion.

In 1900, the regiment went under canvas for the first time, thus doing away with the joking title of the Feather-bed Hussars, whom they were sometimes called. This year saw the call to arms following on the outbreak of the Boer War.

A company volunteered under Captain Bromley Davenport, and on the 20th January there was an impressive service in the Lichfield Cathedral, followed by a send-off banquet in the evening. The next day the contingent left, and they continued on active service until Easter, when a further draft of Yeomen were sent out to fill vacancies.

The Imperial Yeomanry were used very successfully in the South African War for scout work and escorting convoys from point to point.

The Staffordshire contingent performed the work of covering the advance of infantry very thoroughly, and it is recorded that never a shot was fired on any company of infantry whose advance the Staffordshire Imperial Yeomanry were guarding. The company could also maintain that they never left a comrade in the lurch, or had one of their number taken prisoner. They suffered, however, severe casualties and losses through the diseases so rife in that country.

The return in June, 1901, was the signal for much rejoicing in the county, in which all joined.

The uniform which had attired so many, and which had been altered so much during the history of the regiment, was changed to khaki, and the troops trained as mounted infantry, but the full dress, consisting of Hussar tunic, busby, with a red bag and white plume, blue pantaloons, and overalls, was retained for state occasions : and a mess dress was added consisting of a blue stable jacket with scarlet stand-up collar and chain epaulettes, blue overalls with double scarlet piping.

July, 1902, saw the two Staffordshire Companies (new 6th and 106th), after hard treking work in the numerous drives that had concluded the war, completing their duties and embarking for England

Twelve glorious years of peace span the bridge between the homeward bound contingent returning from the Boer War in August, 1902, and the fateful August of 1914, when they were mobilised for the Great War.

We shall not follow the fortunes of the Yeomanry right through the Great War from the mobilisation and the stampede of horses at Bishop's Stortford, but content ourselves with a few fragments from the great drive in Palestine. When General Allenby and his army, which included the Staffordshire Yeomanry, drove the combined Turkish, German and Austrian forces in a panic stricken horde between three and four hundred miles across the desert from Jaffa to Aleppo, crushing them utterly and ending the war on the Palestine front.

FINAL CAVALRY OPERATIONS IN PALESTINE AND SYRIA.

" And branded with a blasted worsted spur."—*Kipling.*

The Division marched 83 miles in $38\frac{1}{2}$ hours, and the patrols did more. The march included the passage of a mountain defile. The sun was very hot and many of the horses did not get any water for six hours. This performance on the part of a complete division, arriving at its destination intact, with only a loss of 150 horses, may constitute a record in the history of cavalry.

Leaving Sarona at 4 a.m. on the 19th September, 1918, the Division passed through the gap made by the XXIst Corps in the enemy's line and marched to the foot of the low line of hills dividing the plain of Sharon from that of Esorhelon. After a halt of 2 hours the Division then crossed the range by the Musmus Pass, which, in ancient times was traversed by the Romans and their armies. After an all-night march, Lejjan, the Megiddo of the Bible, was reached without casualties at daybreak.

The famous plain of Esorhelon was crossed, and the 2nd Lancers, acting as advance guard, charged a hostile body in the way, killing many with the lance and capturing others. El Afuleh, the most important railway junction of the Turks, right in the rear of the centre of their army, was in the hands of the Division by 7 a.m. on the 20th, and all railway communications intercepted. After a few hours rest, the Division marched along the valley of Jezreel to Beisan, its ultimate destination.

In this march, right round the rear of the Turkisk Army,

many captures were made, and the spoils were approximately :

	Prisoners. Officers.	Other Ranks.
Turks	231	7,337
Germans	92	310

There was no opposition ; it was due to the rapidity of their movements everywhere. Their appearance was so unexpected that the enemy was unable to organise a resistance, and threw down their arms in panic.

The 21st Corps of Infantry made this cavalry advance possible. They captured all the enemy's first line positions at Jul Keram, which guarded the Nablus Road and took many prisoners.

The 20th Corps advanced on the right of the 21st Corps in co-operation with Major-General Chaytor's Force in the Jordan Valley, which latter captured Kabr-Said and El Bagalat. The Cavalry Division on the right of the 4th Division captured Nazareth, and further south the Australian Mounted Division took Jenin and 5,000 prisoners.

It appeared as if the destruction of the Turkish Army was complete, and that was the task the British Army set out to do. A later report gave—Total prisoners 30,000 approximately. Nablus captured.

Of the above record the Staffs. Yeomanry took no unimportant part, as their battle honours portray.

The above summary goes to prove what practically constitutes a war record, at all events, in the Eastern theatre of the War.

Note.—There were 3,000 additional prisoners, unsorted, making approximately a total of 11,000. Rifles 315, machine guns 60, motor cars 7, aeroplanes 4, (for the second time in Yeomanry history) treasure chests 1, battery waggons 2, 15 c.m. guns 3, ammunition 15 c.m. 58, trucks 48, coaches 17, locomotives 10, railmotors 7, motor cycles 2. The above were actually brought in.

Horses 1,000, donkeys 250, camels 20.

Grain stores and supplies at Kerkur, Shumrah, El Afuleh, and Beisan, together with large quantities of miscellaneous stores, were all taken.

Note.—Place of the Staffordshire Yeomanry always on the right of the line.

Note.—One Yeoman found in an old ruin an old leather bag full of beautiful Hebrew gold coins in perfect condition.

Extracts from a Letter from Military Hospital, Alexandria, January 9th, 1918.

In taking over from the lines things got very lively. The Turks the previous evening had captured the lines, pack horses and rations, and probably this had got the Turks tail up.

At any rate they attacked and took a hill from "C" Squadron, and we lost pretty heavily.

Brewitt and Noakes were mortally wounded, and Griffiths (once Sergeant, now 2nd Lieut.) was hit through the arm.

Sergt. Burt was killed (shot through the throat).

Sergts. Moore and Bradburn were badly wounded as well as many men.

Old Merriman, the barber, is in the Turk's hands, as well as several others whose names I cannot remember.

Fatty Hammond (he is a signaller now, and no more hard working man lives) got about six bullets in him, and smiled at the Doctor as he remarked that he would not be digging latrines for some time.

Brewitt struggled in using a rifle as a crutch ; he has since died in Ranlah Hospital. He was hit in the stomach, poor chap.

Poor old Noakes could not be found for some time, but Tom Fradley went out and found him. Fradley lay out with Noakes under fire for more than an hour. Noakes had his thigh smashed and died the same night after being under Wadi. Poor old Noakes, our sturdy chap.

The horses had been sent back to Ludd, and we were left here as Infantry, less the horse holders and depleted numbers by casualties and sickness.

The Turks attacked us all along the line, and shifted various units from different positions. They had now troops—storm troops —and they were not half bad either.

On this day I remember old Joe Severn got hit in the throat and Sergt. Freasley in the wrist. In the evening we got orders to attack at dawn and get back the hill we had lost the day previously. We set out in the dark and got part of the ground back. About 7 a.m. the Colonel was hit on the side of the head by a rifle bullet. Sergt. Ballance, I remember, got one through the shoulder, and many of the others stopped one too.

Kennerley, a signaller of " D," was killed, and I went over to him as I thought he had a helio, and we were short of these valuable instruments. I was about the only one moving just at this time, and cannot say whether they actually shot at me, but the bullets pinged and smacked like the crack of a whip on the rocks all about us. One does not mind rifle fire much. Well, the poor chap had not got a helio but only a flag. In going back they got me. I felt something burn my left leg as though a red hot poker had been inserted, and then knew I was touched. I was greatly relieved to find I could walk and had a field dressing put on and again went out. This was November 28th. We had to go back, the Turks pushed the Brigade back on our right, and we had to go too. Fittle White was killed (shot through the heart) after making a most gallant fight. He was the last man to leave his position, and a bullet struck him as he left, killing him instantly. We were scrapping all day, and a terrible job it was getting back to shorten the line. This day the Lincolns lost pretty heavily. Crow and Wright were both killed. Paddison, the Quartermaster, was killed. Holmes, the Chaplain, was in action with them and behaved most gallantly. He accounted for three Turks, and then was himself wounded. We spent two more days in the lines with orders to counter attack with the bayonet if the Turks gained any local success. We had to hold on at any cost until the Infantry got up, their whole flank depended on it. We were a very attenuated line indeed, but worthy our job, and " D" Division have something to be proud of. The Infantry relieved us at last. They had been marching with steam up, and immediately put about four times the number of rifles we had into the line, and a ding-dong fight went on here for about two weeks after we left. We went about 7 miles back and bivouaced.

We must have looked a pitiable lot, men limping, hands bound up with septic sores, boots worn out, and clothing in rags.

The next day the horses came up from Ludd, and this finished me. I could not ride. We went further back to our place of rest out of sound of guns, etc., and I travelled in a sand cart.

On December 2nd, I was sent to Ranlah Hospital, which is a French Convent. There in the garden close to Neil Primrose's grave lie Noakes and Brewitt.

It took me six days to get here, and when I got here I was put to bed, where I remained about ten days, while my wound was dressed and looked after.

I am A.I. now and being boarded to-day, and expect to go to Kantara in a few days en route for the Regiment.

The above extract is not intended to be lightly read, but to be treated as sacred to the dead, and to show some of the sufferings our men, some still serving, went under.

The War over, the Regiment recommenced its annual training at Rhyl. This was the scene of the first Yeomanry Camp after the War, under Major Mander, in the absence of Lieut.-Col. Sir Charles Wiggin, who, however, managed to join the regiment for its drum-head service and read the Lessons. The glorious full dress had now completely vanished, but the mess dress, consisting of blue stable jacket with scarlet stand-up collar, etc., spurs, silver buttons and white gloves, was worn for walking out and on important social occasions ; it being considered one of the most distinctive and smartest uniforms the Yeomanry ever wore.

The curious title of " Mad-mans " was given to the white overalls worn during stables, and much joking was heard in association with them. Occasionally, in stables, were worn the old red forage caps with a large Stafford Knot on one side.

The next year saw the training again in the county, and Himley Park being the scene of regimental activity, thousands took the op-portunity of visiting the regiment in camp on Sports Day, Whit-Monday. In the glorius weather, under the beautiful trees of Lord

Dudley's estate, near the village so full of kind-hearted people, this camp will ever remain a great memoir to Yeoman, who served here ; a memory tinged with sadness, for Himley now has its Garden of Memory, and wind-blown apples fall lightly on to the grave of a noble Yeoman's lady.   Now the task of dipping into the fragments of this famous regiment's past is nearly over, and it would be meet to end it on one of the " glad nights " of the regiment, when the recruits are thrilled to hear the veterans sing their old song again that was once sung on the eve of departure for South Africa :

" Dear old pals, jolly old pals," etc.

Writing of songs reminds one of the great air that so nobly interprets :

The Yeomen of England.
" No other land could nurse them,
But their Mother Land, Old England.
And on the broad bosom
May they ever thrive."

The mounted band of the Staffordshire Yeomanry was trained for many years by the famous John Gladman, who arranged the Regimental March or quick trot, " St. Patrick's Day," and selected his musicians from the Lichfield Troop.

Note.—Among the regimental plate is the huge silver-gilt centre-piece presented by Colonel Heath in 1900 as an acknowledgement of the many happy years he spent in the Yeomanry.

THE OLD HOUSES, BUSINESSES, AND STREETS OF THE BOROUGH.

Stafford is dominated by its picturesque Castle, which lies south-west of the borough and forms for the townsfolk an excellent weather guage, as the storms blow up from the south-west, so the clouds gather over the Castle, telling of coming bad weather.

The irregular streets of the borough, running in from the surrounding districts, all converge on the one bottle-necked main street, whose centre is the Market Square.   This square is the hub, not only of the town's activities, but of the county's.

From this one street branch off many dangerous, narrow thoroughfares, which thread the town and wind about like the very river itself.   One definite end to the main street is at the Public Library where the road forks, whilst the Gaol Square, or Sydney Square, brings up the other.   Extend it cannot, thus cramming most of the shopping area into this one street and its side-shoots.

It is needless to say that there is much ancient lore centred round these old streets and buildings, so let us pause for a moment and dwell on the past of Sydney Square.   The new clock, which has just been erected in this centre, is the successor to a fountain that was placed on the same site in memory of Alderman Thomas Sydney.

He was one of Stafford's most illustrious sons, and became Lord Mayor of London. His shield was affixed to the fountain attached to the base of the old clock. It displayed 13 oak trees, and was surmounted by a hedge-hog, while the motto underneath had its first portion torn away, leaving only " eo agere " for the curious to guess its meaning.

To-day the name Sydney Square is scarcely heard, though the name Sydney House can be seen high up on an adjoining shop.

Adjacent to this building is an edifice that adds interest to the old square. At the beginning of North Walls still stands the former King Edward VI. Grammar School, a structure of faced stone, with a tablet recording its former scholastic use and origin, as follows :

" Free Grammar School.
James Turnock, Esqr.,
Mayor, June, 1813."

Gaol Square garage opposite occupies a site with historical associations, and it is on record that during excavations carried out there many years ago a number of headless skeletons were found, as if they had been thrown into a pit.

The discovery led to many conjectures. Were they the bodies of criminals who had died in the old House of Correction, and their heads severed and given to the surgeons for study, or were they those of priests who suffered torture during religious persecution

A generally accepted theory is that the heads were thrust on the spikes of the Old Foregate, or Northgate, as it was then known, which stood a few yards away from the Trumpet Hotel.

Running between the Elephant and Castle Inn and the probable site of the Old House of Correction is Bull Hill, a name, the origin of which one can only guess. Was bull-baiting practiced there, or was it the recognised place were bulls were tethered at the May Fair ? This is only a tithe of the romance and history of Stafford's ancient square.

Proceeding up Gaolgate one comes across the entrance to a narrow thoroughfare known as Stafford Street, formerly known as Jerningham's Row. There was originally a confectionery shop on the corner noted for the sale of a speciality in cakes named " Stafford Wiggs," the making of which confection had been carried out in Stafford for ages. These cakes were introduced into England from our colonies in France, and were termed " Wygges." They took the form of a thick three-cornered bun, with carraway seeds, the top well sugared and browned in the baking, being usually buttered before eating.

Alterations to this building recently revealed it " wattle and daub " construction, and showed that it had practically no foundation.

Anyone entering the narrow thoroughfare from Gaolgate can see the old open sewer pipes which formerly carried the waste from the adjacent building into the street, whence it found its way into the sewer or kennel, running down through the centre of Gaolgate.

The house with these gulleys is a half-timbered structure with a base of sandstone, and it bows out into the street. The interior is said to contain a powder closet. That fact is uncertain, and a more interesting and concrete fact is the age of the building—its title deeds go back to Stuart days, and refer to Gaolgate as Cow Street. It contains magnificent cellars with stone vaulting.

Higher up this street are traces of cobbles that once lined the road, while a few still remain along the gutters with tiny blades of grass poking up here and there.

A cobbled carriage-way runs off here, leading to the backs of the houses fronting Gaolgate, and running parellel to it. Here before the days of fire brigades, an insurance company housed its private manual up this carriage-way, at the top of which was a back entrance to a private mad house, kept by Dr. Masfen.

The rotten dens and galleries were still in evidence up to the time of the present demolition, and to inspect them was like walking into a Dickensian atmosphere. This house contained a very fine old oak staircase leading to a completely panelled room, with a carved border, quaint hinges on the panelled doors, twisted iron grates, while wide oak boards covered the floor.

Underneath the house is honeycombed with cellars and secret places. The most interesting discoveries consist of the opening up in the basement of the mouth of an ancient stone well, 22 feet deep, with 5 feet of water still in it.

A crude lead pipe runs down one side of this well, of unmortared blocks of stone, and is protected at the bottom by a small block of wood attached, to prevent mud being syphoned up with the water. This pipe communicates with an ordinary pumping well, from which early householders obtained their water.

It is curious that behind the old stone well is another, similar in size, containing 1 foot less of water, and composed of red bricks, while behind this is still another well, but filled in and dry.

The next discovery of interest was of an old panelled door near the fireplace of the drawing room, plastered on the outside, and leading on to the almost flat roof of a passage, extending three yards, at the end of which curiously enough is a pair of sliding bottle-glass windows on the adjacent " Dolphin " Inn.

What secrets does this old entrance hold ?

How easy for some Jacobite plotter to arrive in Stafford on one of the many old coaches that used to pull up at the " Dolphin " and take a room on the first floor, slide the windows back, and step across on to the roof of the passage described, creep along and gain admittance through the secret door to a rendezvous in the heart of the adjoining house, unknown to servants or enemies.

Higher up on the Dolphin wall shows a considerable portion of the ancient " wattle and daub " used to fill up in between the beams by early builders.

The position of these beams shows also that the " Dolphin " formerly overhung the street.

This old posting establishment, with a figure of a dolphin as a sign, must have been built before the next house, as they seemed not to have built a wall of their own but simply knocked out a hole here and there on the " Dolphin " wall, to let their roughly adzed beams in.

The deeds still extant go back to the year 1642, when on the 13th of August the property passed from George Cradock, Esq., to Wolfran Smith, M.D. The deeds opens with the usual " Year of the reign of our Sovereign Lord Charles by the grace of God," etc., etc. On October 4th, 1656, the property passes from Wolfran Smith to John Wilson, who writes, " And I give to such poor as shall come to my funeral, not inhabiting in Stafford, the sum of three pounds to be distributed to them in bread."

Outhouses that belonged to the firm of grocers, Messrs. Debac and Sheaf, still exist, a little further on, and only just recently a door with their name emblazoned thereon was removed.

A very old resident of Stafford can remember his father telling him how he slept under the counter as an apprentice and finally ran away to sea.

Almost immediately opposite stands the quaintly-named Slipper Inn, and at the other end of this interesting street is the " Jolly Crafts," with its ample accommodation for the country folk with their carts and floats.

Its present name is derived from Lord Stafford, who is Lord of the Manor, and owns considerable property in the street. It has, at some period, also rejoiced in the name of Lewis Lane.

This brings one to Mount Street, which runs round into Gaol Square again. The street-widening that has lately been in progress in Mount Street, which partially encircles an old fashioned garden, sweeps away most of the remaining traces of an old fortification within the town walls of Stafford, known as the Mount. The remains consist of a sandstone wall about 5 feet high, composed of enormous blocks of sandstone, each one weighing as much as 1½cwts., and even 2cwts., and dressed only on the one side, the wall encircling much higher ground than the street, showing that the garden was artifically made. From the fact of the wall only being dressed on one side, and the many large stones that the workmen constantly unearthed, there had been apparently another half of the wall making it, when in its original use, a yard in width. The workmen, during their excavations, have not discovered any relics of former times, not even coping stones of the old wall, though certain smaller, but unmoulded stones found about, may have helped to form battlements. There is scarcely any foundation, and thus, through the centuries, the wall had leaned further and further out into the street, until it reached a dangerous angle with, of course, its superstructure of brickwork added many years ago. Faint traces of the masons' marks appear in the beds of some of the larger stones, but the most interesting marks are at the end of the wall where there was formerly a doorway. The door, which one can imagine was a heavy, iron studded, oaken affair, closed in a groove of heavy flanged stones, and its latch and lock fastened in a mighty stone with the holes let in to accommodate them. On the outside of the groove are clearly seen the cuts where the soldiers sharpened their arms and arrows. These marks are the more interesting because neither St. Mary's nor St. Chad's shows any signs of these grooves, which are fairly common up and down the country ; the Parish Church at Penkridge being the nearest local example.* These stones have been preserved.

About the history of the Mount itself very little is known ; the name Mount, of course, was sometimes applied to a small fortification of this character, such as the Brass Mount in the Tower of London. There is a Mount in York Castle, while Mount St. Michael is well-known to all.

Perhaps it was the old Castle that we read of, as built within the walls of the town, or again it may have been the substantial stronghold where the early Stafford coins were minted.

The garden, which has for many years occupied the site, is a very old one, as witness the mulberry tree. The huge rockeries and quaint arches, with their attendant grotesques, are not coeval with the wall, but were carted there from the Parish Church at the time of Sir Gilbert Scott's restoration of St. Mary's in 1840.

The sandstone that composed the wall of the Mount evidently came from the old quarry on Kingston Hill, as did also the stone from which St. Chad's Church was built.

Back into Gaolgate again, through Stafford Street, and directly opposite we come to the old " Three Tuns," which, many years ago, was the club house for a curious ladies' society that flourished in Stafford. About 1850 there existed a society originating from Wolverhampton called " The Reformed Order of Old Women." The first headquarters was at the Abercrombie Inn, and had a membership of 100 sisters. They had their own surgeon attached to the lodge, who, on appointment, offered to attend them free for a quarter, and presented them with six gallons of ale. It was agreed that " the Lodge meet every other week, that 8d. per member be paid each Lodge night for sick benefits, and 2d. each member besides, which shall be spent in ale." Those present consuming the allowance of those absent as well as their own !

There was only one male in the society, and he was the Secretary, who was voted a salary of 15s. per quarter and a share of the ale. Later on the society was moved to the Cock Inn, in Eastgate, and finally to the Three Tuns in Gaolgate. Here the society became more respectable and a lot of the drinking was eliminated, it probably being too noticable here.

*Some grooves have since been discovered in the walls of St. Thomas' Priory.

Let us leave this old fashioned building with its quaint old arch, under which the carts go up the yard, and the sweet clubable sisters, and poke further along the interesting buildings that line the ancient thoroughfare.

It was in Thorn's establishment, in whose spacious cellars they stored the Assize wine, when George the second was King in 1744. Opposite is Messrs. Cliffs, established in 1795. This business still proudly uses the original spice canisters over a century old. Cheek by jowl is Geo. Masons, Ltd., with its rambling passages and oak-panelled rooms, tiny closets and wainscotted chambers.

Holding it up on the other side is Wilks, the florist, and between the two buildings, hidden by courses of masonry ,are carved beams and projections, the whole of which are carved with beautiful flowers and foliage ; the ancient wood-carver must have known that this was the place for flowers, for the fine specimens of his craft, hidden to all but the rats, vie with that glorious profusion of flowers that fill the windows, and gladden by their fresh presence many a dark gloomy day and cheer the passers-by with their sweet fragance. The roses which cluster in vases on the glass shelves owe their support to a hidden piece of English oak, marked with the adze, and smothered with the Tudor rose, both single and double.

The mediæval wood carver must have thought that this part of the main street needed brightening by roses ; and so we think to-day. Look above to the roof of the building, and see the quaint old dormer window that crowns the building, with its slated sides and leaded panes, through which the wind whistles like a hundred ghosts. What an odd, old piece ; the other part of the building was re-built some years ago, and, upon the walls being stripped in one room, a very fine piece of oak panelling was discovered. Practically all the rooms are wainscotted, and the floors were composed of very wide oak boards. Two fine black oak staircases, with Jacobean bannisters, led to the third and fourth storeys. A fire grate, in a top storey room, with circular bars, was very quaint, with a carved black oak frame. A good deal of " wattle and daub " was found between the timbers and a lot of bricks was composed of unburnt clay mixed with straw.

Many feet below the floor of the old sandstone cellar is gravel which has the appearance of having formed, at some remote period, the bed of a river.

We pass on to the Market Square, mention having already been made to Dr. Masfen's Madhouse, it having, probably the finest staircase in Stafford.

Sam Johnson's shoe shop has been on its present site for generations, and together with the Elizabethan House and Mummery's, the jewellers, on the corner, was burnt to the ground in the great fire of Stafford 45 years ago.

Jewellery has been sold at the corner shop as far as records go back. Averills, the chemists, on the other side of the Square, has also been in the same family for many years, the structure dating from 1474.

In the Market Square is the entrance to the Market Hall. Several of the old stall-holders can remember standing in the Market Square and down Market Street, sixty years ago, before this present structure was built. Facing the square stands the oldest banking establishment in the town, that of Lloyd's Bank, whose commencement in the year 1737 as Stephenson, Salt and Co., carries us back to the reign of the early Georges again.

Formerly the porter of the bank wore the peacock crest of the Salt's on his buttons. The Salt family, who lived at Weeping Cross house, were for long closely identified with the life of the town, and to one of them is due the founding of the Salt Library, with its rare and valuable collections.

An older institution than the bank, however, was the old Liberal Club, whose existence went back even unto Cromwellian times. The oldest established trade in Stafford is that of tanning, going back 300 years. Further along the street is Allen's, established 1840, whilst the " Staffordshire Advertiser " was established about 1794, when George III. was King.

Morgan's, the wine merchants, was founded in 1780, which reminds one of the inns of the town which date back to very early days, like the Vine, the Swan, the Bear, and others of the same trade.

Marson's, the chemists, founded about 1832, with prescription books going back to 1848, the foundations are extremely old and of local sandstone ; Brookfields, established 1743 ; Dale's, about 1800 ; and the Tannery, 1630.

The Lyceum, at Stafford, was an old Patent Theatre, which freed it from the annual application to the Justices of the Peace for a renewal of its license, founded in George III's reign. Linkmen were used after the theatre until 1896.

There are dozens of other old business establishments, those recorded being but a scanty list of the whole. Information about them generally is rather difficult to get hold of, but it is interesting to show how long the traders of Stafford have satisfactorily served the needs of the inhabitants.

Among the very interesting features that stand out high up on the old business premises and houses are the ancient fire marks. These marks, about one foot high, made of copper, and originally smart, gilded affairs, were placed on houses by the old private insurance companies to denote insured premises. They are now very faded, and hardly discernable, but at one time they played an important part in the life of the town. These insurance companies were practically unknown before the Great Fire of London, when that colossal catastrophy made men devise some means of mutual protection against the common enemy fire, by forming private companies. They maintained their own firemen and equipment, although the State had passed an Act compelling all parishes to keep axes, helmets, syringes, etc.   Apparantly the parish equipment did not meet the needs of the private companies, with much wooden property at risk, so they maintained their own fire-fighting appliances.   One local branch of either " The Sun " or the " Norwich Union " Insurance Company kept their private manual at the back of Stafford Street.

At the stirring clang of the old fire bell, from its cradle on the roof of the Guild Hall, the gangs of firemen belonging to all the local insurance companies in the town would immediately rush in the direction of the building on fire.   They, of course, would either be guided to the fire by the people who gave the alarm, or by the glare or smoke of the fire.   No streets had name-plates, and if it happened that firemen belonging to the Sun office reached the fire first, only to discover from the fire mark on the burning building that the premises were insured by the Norwich Union, they would, instead of commencing to help quell the outbreak, stand by and look on and jeer their business rivals when they came panting up late to the scene. This course of action was taken to show the insured how much more alert and efficient they were in times of fire than any other insurance company.   A much more important significance was attached to the fire marks, however, for in bad times when riots were common, like the bread riots in Stafford, the inflamed mob would often foregather round the building of one against whom they perhaps may have had a fancied grievance, and threaten to burn down the shuttered premises.   The presence of the fire mark would stay their hand, for they would say among themselves " what is the good of firing the house of an insured man.   It would not harm him," so the building would be safe for both insurers and insured.   Some fire marks have the number of the insured's policy on the base, but this is not so on the Stafford fire marks.   They are principally the " Brittanic," " The County," and the " Norwich Union " (founded 1797).   The latter company's marks predominate in the town.   They all show the crest or badge of the company with the name on the base.   Norwich Union fire marks are on houses in Salter Street and Eastgate.   There is one over Messrs. Dobson's shop in Greengate, Walmsley's in Gaolgate has the simple word " Union " on its front, while the Ancient High House has a mark, black with age, hardly decipherable, with " County " on the base.   These marks were always placed high up out of the reach of thieves.

The following extract is from an article originally published in the Staff Magazine of Lloyds Bank, and gives some details of Stafford's connection with the origin of the banking business.

" In the year 1737, John Stevenson, a mercer in the town, with remarkable foresight and enterprise forsook the haberdashery business to follow what was then a novel and intriguing occupation, that of banking.   For it must be remembered that this was a very early date for an undertaking of this kind outside London, and Macleod in his 'Dictionary of Political Economy ' states that in the year 1750 there were not more than twelve banks outside the Metropolis.

"Stevenson, whose bank was known as the Stafford Old Bank, died in the year 1777, and Aris's "Birmingham Gazette," of March in that year speaks of him as 'an eminent banker of Stafford.' On his death the bank passed into the hands of his son, William, who also founded a bank at 85, Cheapside, in the Citp of London, in the year 1788. William Stevenson had, besides other children, a son, John, and a daughter, Sarah. The latter in 1800 married her cousin, John Stevenson Salt, thus bringing the Salt family into the business. John Stevenson was placed in the Stafford Bank and John Salt in the London business, which was known as that of Messrs. Stevenson and Salt. The Webb family, about this time acquired an interest of the Stafford Bank and remained partners for many years, long after the original Stevenson family had dropped out with the deaths of John in 1802 and his father, William, in 1807. Eventually the Webb family ceased its connections with the bank and John Stevenson Salt's eldest son, Thomas, joined him in the bank at Stafford while his younger sons went into the business in London. It is a curious fact that the two banks were kept quite separate and never amalgamated. The London firm of Stevenson, Salt and Company moving from Cheapside to 80, Lombard Street, at the signs of "The Haunch of Venison' and 'The Three Herrings' and 'The Civet Cat,' a curious mixture, crossed the road to number 20, and there amalgamated with Messrs. Bosanquet, Beechcroft and Reeves, of No. 73 in the street, the new firm being known as Bosanquet, Salt, and Company. In 1884 they joined forces with Barnett, Hoares, Hanbury, and Lloyd, of Nos. 60 and 62, and with Lloyds Bank Company of the Midlands, to become part of what is now Lloyds Bank Limited. In the meantime, to return to the Stafford Bank, the latter had continued to flourish, and in the year 1866 amalgamated with the newly-formed Lloyds Banking Company of Birmingham, thus dating its connection with our bank some twenty years earlier than that of its London counterpart, though both were destined to join forces at least under the same banner.

John Stevenson apparently took a great interest in his Stafford Bank, and a letter of his, written on the 5th of June, 1802, to London, is well worth persuing in these days of mail robberies, since it refers to the risk of moving bank notes in any quantity, the Bank having at the time its own private notes. The letter reads :—
' When I came from London I brought with me about £6,000 in £5 notes. I believe when you come down you generally bring a larger sum, which I think is very hazardous to do in a Post Chaise in the neighbourhood of London. I mention this circumstance as I imagine you are not acquainted with the largeness of the sum you are in the habit of bringing down. If you could make it convenient to come in one of the coaches as far as Northampton once or twice in the year I think there would be little danger the rest of the way. Or we

might have them sent down at less risque in trusses by the waggon directed to Mr. James Webb about £2,000 at a time. For my own part I think the risque attending these notes returning from London is very great indeed as they are payable to Bearer on demand and consequently irrecoverable. I should have no objection to pay a considerable sum annually to be ensured from it. I think if I were to determine I should do as Mr. Cobb does, not issue any. The profit upon them I am fully convinced is not equal to the risque of bringing them back across such places as Finchley Common and Hounslow Heath in a Post Chaise.'

Opposite the Swan Hotel, with its memories of George Borrow, who was ostler there, and Charles Dickens, who spent a gloomy evening within its walls, stands the famous old church of St. Chad's.

A quaint old custom is carried out twice a year by the Verger of this church. Each Christmas Eve, this functionary proceeds to an old house in the parish formerly known as the Turk's Head and proceeds to collect from the owner a sum of ten shillings. This sum is half the tithe on the property, and with five shillings of this expended in loaves of bread, the Verger returns to the Church as the evening draws near. Donning his robe of office, the dexterous Verger then rings the Church bell to announce to the Borough that Hale's Charity, as it is called, is about to be doled out to the needy. In file the recipients, and receive according to their needs the Staff of Life. The custom is repeated on Easter Eve, while the Wardens receive the other five shillings for church repairs, and this has been carried out regularly for 289 years.

" John Stevenson Salt died in 1845, being well-known in banking circles. Thomas Salt, his son succeeded him as head of the Stafford banking business and was eventually joined in it by his son Thomas (who was created a Baronet in 1899).

The local branch of the Manchester and District Bank recently celebrated its 100 years existence in Stafford.

THE OLD HOUSE OF CORRECTION AND COUNTY GAOL.

> " O'er all there hung the shadow of a fear,
> A sense of mystery, the spirit daunted,
> And said, as plain as a whisper in the ear,
> The place is haunted !"
> W. H. Ainsworth and his Friends.

The empty barrack of a building that runs the length of Gaol Road with its flanking brick towers is now a thing of the past, and no customers left. The first mention ever made of a Gaol in Stafford was in the Pipe Rolls of 1189-90, and was apparently situated at the end of Crowberi Lane (Crabbery Street). Ancient stonework of this old prison still exists behind the present Wesleyan Church, Near here too, are portions of the old Deanery, incorporated in the structure of the present Noah's Ark Inn.

The Deans of St. Mary's had the power of Justiciary over the community they ruled, and the Gaol was possibly part of their domain, they also had a drowning pit for women, between St. Mary's and the top of Averill's entry, and a gallows for males.

No doubt offenders of importance would be lodged in the dungeons of Stafford Castle until they were put on trial, or kept there to rot for their lives.

This old prison was taken down in the year 1700, and for the next 94 years was located in the Gaol Square, the old Northgate being used for that purpose. It was known as the House of Correction.

It would probably resemble the gate at Winchester, now a museum, which was at that time used as a prison, as well as a gate to the town. The Winchester Gate has guns mounted on the battlements and peering through the embrasures, and has a condemned cage for prisoners about to be executed. The Stafford executions took place in a field near the Sandeford brook, beyond the walls at that date.

Anyone who has seen the Gatehouse at Winchester can thus get some idea of the Foregate or North-Gate of Stafford.

There were 65 males confined here, apart from females, the terrible condition of whom was the cause of the New County Gaol being built in Gaol Road in 1794.

Of course, as the population increased, the prison accommodation had not moved along with it and debtors were incarcerated in the free ward or county chamber.

The new Gaol is now exactly as when built, and the place of execution was moved to outside the main entrance, where the Governor's House now stands. This has served the county for a prison ever since and its accommodation has never failed. During the Great War, it was turned into a Military Prison and, after then, was closed. One of its buildings is a very fine Church of England, with some beautiful carving on the altar executed by Borstal boys.

There is little difference between this Church and any other, except for the raised seats along the sides, where the Warders followed the service with one eye, and watched their charges with the other.

At the west of the Church were two special pews for condemned murderers.

Remains of the rods can still be seen where curtains were ranged round each one, so that the prisoner and his guards could neither see or be seen, but could hear all and join in the service if they wished.

No one, therefore, saw the condemned man, and, if there were two, they would be brought in separately, so that they would be unaware of each other's presence in the Chapel, one on one side and the other in the adjacent pew.

Such prisoners were brought in at the back of the Church, just after the service had started.

The execution sheds, with green doors, the whole of which looks like a garage, can be clearly seen from the upper windows of the Governor's House, so that on execution morning, the Governor used to go up and lock the doors of these rooms until all was over. The view would include the procession from the condemned cell to the execution shed, and also the Sheriff, warders, and other witnesses ranged ready to witness the ceremony. At Stafford the condemned cell was some little distance from the scaffold.

The actual drop where the condemned was placed resembles a cellar door, with highly polished hinges, having a lever at the side similar to a gear lever on a car. The hangsman releases this lever which draws the gleaming well-oiled bolts holding the door, which immediately drops downwards with a noise like a cellar trap-door violently slammed down.

In the porch is the clock which the warder on night duty checks by. There are little pegs on it which he must push in at the appointed time, and the clock, during the day, pushes them out again.

After the execution had taken place, a notice of the fact was posted on the Prison Gate, and a black flag was flown from above the gate, whilst the bell from Christ Church tolled the knowledge to the town.

The body of the executed was then carried up from the cellar below, in which it had been swinging listless as a pendulum. It was removed from the noose with the elastic band, that makes slipping impossible and death instantaneous, by the hangman, who had fastened it on a live man and now takes off a dead one, and taken to the little mortuary to await the jury. That solemn " body " would gaze on that stiff " body," and its verdict would be as having followed the course of the law ! The interment in the prison grounds followed.

Over the execution sheds is the photographer's department, where every new prisoner, on arriving, was photographed, sitting in a curious little chair for that purpose. In this room is also the wheel of the apparatus down below, hidden by a casing, though, of course, they did not tell newcomers this.

Executions were formerly carried out on a movable vehicle, which was trundled just outside the gates and the condemned would walk up the steps from the prison, through the inside of the vehicle, to the top outside, where all could observe him and his entrance into eternity.

The hangman would then serve his usual dirty trick on him, and down would go the body into the inside of the vehicle, and the whole would then be pushed inside again, like a punch and judy show. One of the old warders had a piece of this vehicle and also one of the tread boards from the old tread mill, formerly in full working order, as would have delighted Mr. Scrooge, which was used in this prison. The worn marks of feet show the service it had done.

The old Black Maria, which everyone can remember, was also

Note.—A black cap is used at the sentence of death to shroud the Judge, and a white one at the execution to cover the condemned.

parked here, when not in use, to transport the prisoners. It was fitted with little box-like cells, and the guards sat on view behind, from the Police Station or the Assize Court to the Prison, etc.

The maze of buildings, which included portions for female prisoners as well as males, and occasionally children, born in this prison, whose birth certificate would simple give a number in Gaol Road, Stafford, which gave no indication of the child being born in prison. Spacious workshops, a hospital, with its loathsome padded cells, Governor's offices, the Roman Catholic Chapel, and other places, all help to make up this huge buildings, surrounded by its high curtain wall, defended by brick towers, where the warders lived, and the gate-house with its big notice-board outside, containing a list of dire penalties for those who would assist a prisoner to escape.

This gateway has windows so heavily barred that the light must have a difficulty in piercing the interior ; whilst the large gate has a little wicket with ponderous knocker and grated grille, and has altogether a very repellant atmosphere.

Extract.

" The Autobiography of a Crook."

By " Netley Lucas."

" I worked in the garden all day. One of my beloved poets has said something to the effect that man is nearer to God in a garden than anywhere else on earth. I found it so. A great calm descended upon me, and when about 4 p.m. I was locked up for the night I was quite resigned to my fate, although within a few yards of the ' window ' of my cell was the execution shed, a hideous little brick building from which they launch the souls of murderers into eternity. I remember thinking to myself that execution sheds should be made beautiful—stained glass windows, Gothic arches, and so forth—for though the law condemns a man's body to ignominious death and corruption, there is something about him which transcends the authority of man-made law, and this something should, I think, be liberated with some beautiful ceremonial from its poor clay prison house."

PALMER, THE POISONER, AND OTHER ROGUES.

" Therefore behoveth him a full long spoon,
That shall ete with the fiend."—*Chaucer.*

Stafford is very fortunate in never having given birth to any infamous criminals, assassins, fanatics or other malefactors such as have disgraced the reputations of many other noble towns, and who have caused quite a lot of suffering in the world and have done no one, except lawyers, any good. Probably she has always seen too much of other town's rogues to want any of her own, and the sentences meted out at the Assize courts and the punishments in which the town did not lack variety, were sufficient to keep our townsfolk in the narrow paths of rectitude.

There are three rogues of which some account must be given, as they became intimately connected with Stafford, and they are, —first, Stephen Dugdale, a bailiff ; second, Richard Vaughan, a Stafford linen draper who first forged bank of England notes ; and third, William Palmer, a doctor, practicing at Rugeley, who poisoned one person after another.

Quite an interesting trio to link together, one will agree—an embezzler, a forger, and a poisoner, but not one sordid and commonplace. All three are original, well-known and accomplished, Dugdale more particularly as a liar than anything else.

Let us first take Dugdale, who is in the employ of the Aston family of Tixall Hall. It is in the reign of Charles II., and the scare of a Popish plot is filling the air with wild alarms, and dreadful tales are circulating amongst honest men. Stephen is a bailiff employed by Lord Aston, and, having embezzled a lot of money belonging to his master, escapes, only to fall into the hands of soldiers watching all the roads from the house. The Romish sympathies of Lord Aston, and it being well known that his house was a retreat for them, had occasioned this military measure. Dugdale is taken into Stafford and confined in the North Gate, being carefully guarded until his interrogation. It is in this old fortification that, with his guilty bag of gold, he is first set face to face with the infamous Dr. Titus Oates.

This terrible informer was in the act of scouring the country for further evidence against the Catholics and he realised, on seeing Dugdale, that here was the very man he was looking for in his designs against the Catholics of this country. Dugdale is closely questioned and then subjected to three or four days of solitary confinement in the foul, loathsome dungeon of the House of Correction, and at the conclusion he gathers that to obtain freedom, and pardon, he must be the mouth-piece of manufactured evidence against his employer, whom he has already greatly wronged. He accordingly makes a declaration, on oath, to the delighted Oates, that he has overheard a plot in Tixall Hall to kill the King and has seen treasonable letters to that effect. On this sworn statement Lord Aston was impeached, and lodged in the Tower, and several others were committed to the Gaol in Stafford, so recently occupied by Dugdale.

They included one Peters, a priest named Cotton, and George Hobson, a tenant of Lord Stafford, the firm Catholic friend of Lord Aston. Some were imprisoned for uttering treasonable words against his Majesty, and others for stirring up sedition.

In February, 1679, Dugdale was examined by the King in Council. The emergence from that with flying colours gave Dugdale the confidence to keep refreshing his memory concerning the doings of Tixall Hall and to send one after another to the scaffold. The nation was so scared that people and juries believed anything that

Oates and Dugdale would give testimony to. Everywhere was inflamed, while the history of the terrible gunpowder plot was refreshed in all minds. Even those in the highest circles were suspected, including the Queen herself, who was, of course, a Catholic, Catherine of Bragazna, whose dowry was the island of Tangier, and had brought her own priests, etc., with her.

It is said that later, when King Charles II. was on his death-bed a priest was sent for, but the Queen's confessors could not succour him as they neither spoke or understood English. So Father Huddlestone, the only official Catholic priest in England, allowed to wear a cassock, was summoned, and, being a friar, knew not how to shrive, so that the Queen's confessors had to hurriedly instruct him in Latin.

To return, however, the fear of a plot meant that a person was only to be denounced and conviction automatically followed.

The Chaplain from Tixall flew for his life, but the others were not so successful, and the trials were a parody of justice. Let us not forget that these were the days when black magic was firmly believed in, ignorance and superstition abounded, and coronor's juries would return a verdict of " wilful murder " against an article causing a death ; even animals were known to have been brought to the Bar, to be tried for murder. So minds, whose limitations were such as allowed them to do these things, and considered them quite right, must not be blamed for getting scared over the rumoured plots of a party who might at any moment, blow them out of their beds with gunpowder, or if they gained the reins of government to institute the Bloody Inquisition and Autoda Fé.

They had done all these things and they were indelibly stamped on the minds of the English people to such an extent as to wish for the extermination of all Catholics from the land.

So, in Stafford, Father Gaven, Atkins, and Andrew Bromwich were all sentenced on the testimony of Dugdale to the scaffold, but Atkins died in Stafford Gaol after the trial, probably after languishing in a dungeon polluted by the former presence of Dugdale. The terrible sentence included the most dreadful butchery it was possible to carry out on a fellow creature. No doubt the severance of the parts of the body, following on the cutting down after being partially hanged, would, to the minds of the people, preclude the possibility of the spirits of the wild-eyed condemned ever returning to this earth to haunt the places where their lives had been lived, or to become a token or a signal, or omen, to those who still laboured on in the work for which these partially hanged bodies had hellishly died.

The body was quartered by a large and sharp knife, and then the streaming remains would be lifted up by the means of an immense two pronged flesh fork, and by either the masked executioner or some

Note.—Father Sutton was executed at Stafford in 1587.

Note.—To their minds, probably, it would be a complete obliteration of body and spirit. The Blood of the Martyrs was the Seed of the Church.

other terrible functionary who assisted him, would plunge the quarters of what was once a human being into the cauldrons of oil and tar. How refreshing must have been the smell of the tar against the stench that mingled with the smoke from the fires under the cauldrons. Beneath the scaffold was the halter still swaying. The smoke must have made the scene look as if the earth had cracked in this unhallowed spot, and devils from hell had been spewed up with their bloody prongs, grimacing at the gallows, half naked, and foaming at the mouth, drenched in blood, hell's spawn on earth. Sometimes, when the quarters were not intended for exhibition, they were simply buried at the cross-roads with a stake driven through to prevent the spirit wandering. When, however, the remains were intended as a warning to others, they were placed in cages on a high gibbet, and occasionally recoated with pitch, so that when the flesh rotted away the bones would still be more or less left in position to rattle away on a stormy night and frighten the wayfarer.

Still the country cried out for more victims, and a demand for something more than poor priests was in the air. A pillar, a tower of strength, and an ornament of that hatred church was needed as a terrible example to the humbler followers of the Faith, to satiate the lusts of a temporarily bereft nation. Oates and Dugdale both realised that if they could not keep on bringing forward fresh victims their job was finished, and they would no more be a power in the land ; they would become a back number, or perhaps their enemies might pull hidden wires to bring round the edged tool of the law in their direction, against their guilty selves.

The easiest mark was Lord Stafford, the friend of Lord Aston, one of the weakest of the Catholic group of Lords, one not beloved by other scions of that noble family, and somewhat simple minded.

Lord Stafford was a frequent caller at Tixall Hall during the time that Dugdale was bailiff, and so the rest was easy. The Baron was placed on trial before the House of Lords on the charge of high treason, having elected, as was his right, to be tried by his equals.

Dugdale's evidence before that august Chamber was, that when bailiff at Tixall, one Sunday morning Lord Stafford came to Tixall to hear Mass, and Dugdale went to the outer gate to meet him. He deposed that Lord Stafford promised him £500 to help bring in the Catholic religion ; the King was to be killed. Dugdale consented. (What a tale !). The witness also related treasonable matters heard while concealed behind an oak tree, connected with the proposed death of the King. (Oak trees in Staffordshire seemed always connected with Charles II, as at Boscobel).

The outer gate is the famous Gatehouse, built long before Mary Queen of Scots passed under it, as a close prisoner, to the Hall, and is all that remains of Tixall Hall. The Chapel, where Lord Stafford heard Mass that Sunday morning, has been re-erected at Great Haywood. He little dreamed that the steward who had met him just before, and had ordered a foot-boy to take his Lordship's horse to the stables, was soon to throw the mesh round him, only to be severed by the headman's axe. Even the oak tree has gone, known as Stafford oak, and Oates' Oak. It was destroyed in 1880, leaving only the beautiful Renaissance Gatehouse, with its chimes, as a memorial to the past.

The trial of Lord Stafford lasted six days, when he was found guilty by his peers. The terrible sentence was reduced to simple beheading—a privilege of nobility—by Charles II., in spite of great opposition, the question being raised as to whether the King had the right to do it. To do his duty, Charles was likely to jeopardise himself, and it is curious to notice how often gracious acts of Charles II. are forgotten by people when they sum up his character. It is said that he never said a foolish thing, and never did a wise one, but this and other acts of King Charles show how incorrect this saying was. There is no doubt that Charles lived behind a mask nearly all his life.

So ended the life of Lord Stafford by the headman's axe, and Dugdale himself came to grief in the following year over the trial of Collidge, after which the Crown dispensed with his services. Oates also was finally deposed and imprisoned with the privilege of walking at the tail-end of a cart once a year, with the six-thronged whip of the public tormentor to assist him. Lord Aston languished in the Tower for six years, when he was released by order of Parliament. Aston was a great friend and patron of Izaak Walton. This passes Dugdale from the pages of Stafford rogues, and it is with great relief we leave these pages, soiled by blood and liars.

" Nix my dolly pals fake away."

Richard Vaughan was the cause of as much anxiety and alarm in the hearts of the Governors of the Bank of England and the financial circles of the day as Dugdale caused in his day in the Priest-holes of the Catholic party.

Richard William Vaughan was a linen draper in business at Stafford and was fairly prosperous. This was in the year 1758, round about the time when many of the present business firms in Stafford were started. He was in good circumstances, and apparently the only reason for forging appears to have been that he was in love, and wished to appear wealthier in the eyes of his fiancée than he really was. Love does many strange things we are told, but not often more terrible than the fate of this trader at Stafford, who was hanged at Tyburn for this offence, which was the cause of a new phrase of crime. One of the tickets admitting one person to a seat at the scaffold is still extant. We wonder wheher the young lady sorrowed over the fate of her cavalier, who uttered false notes and laid ill-gotten riches

Note.—The watch that Lord Stafford wore on the scaffold is still treasured by the recent Lord Stafford.

in her lap as a proof of his wealth, and then had to take a jump into eternity ! Perhaps she sighed for

A coach and six,
Six black horses, as black as pitch.

Anyway, the alarm was great to the bank establishment who had circulated paper freely for 64 years, the forgery being so perfect as several artists had been employed on different parts of the work. It was through one of these assistants that the discovery was made, and the first forger of Bank of England notes, to the great satisfaction of everybody, was arrested.

The forging of bank-notes has a fatal fascination for criminals who are expert engravers. Vaughan had, in 1758, with the assistance of several engravers, produced twelve £20 bank-notes. These he handed over to his fiancée as proof of his financial position. The fraud was discovered. He was tried, and as forging bank-notes was then a capital offence, he was sentenced to death by hanging. Shortly afterwards a schoolmaster copied a note with pen and ink. It was a very clever imitation. But his ingenuity did not save him from the hands of the hangsman. It 1802 it was announced in Parliament that, owing to the phenomenal increase in the number of forgeries, the Bank of England found it necessary to engage seventy additional clerks to detect spurious notes. From 1797 to 1805 one hundred and forty-six forgers were hanged. Hanging did not, however, seem to have any effect on the number of prosecutions. Finally, public opinion became so outraged at the frequency of these savage sentences that the extreme penalty was eventually repealed.

Now a glimpse of William Palmer, M.D., of Rugeley, of whom many articles, pamphlets and books have been written, and who has frequently been discribed as one of the most wicked men in the world. Most of his life and his terrible murders are too well-known to need mention here, but it is interesting to record that he was partially trained in the wards of Stafford Infirmary and possibly saw the executions outside the Gaol so near to his work, where this sinister figure was to pay the full price of his own awful crimes. Palmer was a very regular worshipper at St. Mary's Church, Stafford.

The total number of people whom he poisoned can never be known, it included his wife and brother, and was at first entirely without suspicion. Some of the victims lie in the churchyard at Rugeley. One named Cook, whose winnings on the turf Palmer coveted, lies just inside the gate of the new churchyard, with an epitaph, recording that his life was taken away.

When put on trial a special act of Parliament was passed transferring the case to London, owing to the local feeling against the prisoner.

Note.—The Usher calls : Oyes. Oyez. Oyez. My Lords the King's Justices do strictly charge and command all persons to keep silence while sentence of death is passing upon the prisoner at the Bar, upon pain of imprisonment.

God Save The King.

He was sentenced as follows :

" William Palmer, the sentence of the Court is that you shall be taken back to the place from which you have come, and there you shall be hanged by the neck until you are dead, and may God have mercy on your soul. Amen."

Palmer, heavily ironed, and accompanied by the Governor of Stafford Gaol, was brought back to Stafford by train, and taken back to prison, outside of which, the next day, he had to die.

He had already been imprisoned for six months before he was taken before the Central Criminal Courts in London, the delay probably occurring owing to a special act of Parliament having to be passed authorising the transference of the hearing from the Stafford Assizes to London.

When he left Stafford he was accompanied by the Deputy-Governor and a warder, and was not, as is usual for a male prisoner travelling to trial, in any way handcuffed or chained. On Stafford Station the three went into the buffet, where Palmer toasted his companions and joked with the bar-maid.

His return, 13 days later, was at midnight, when, loaded with chains, and with not less a personage than the Governor of Newgate, besides a local superintendent, Palmer was much irritated by his chains which impeded his movements, and he complained to his escort: " Woollaston, I've had a wearying trial of it, twelve long days, bother these chains, I wish they were off."

The next morning, in view of one of the largest crowd gathered together that Stafford has ever known, estimated at twenty or thirty thousand, and controlled by a large body of Dragoons drafted into the town for the purpose, Palmer, to the toiling of the bell in the tower of Christ Church, was brought out to a hushed expectant concourse. This was the 14th June, 1856.

The execution over, and everybody having glutted themselves by the horrible sight, the body was taken back into Gaol. According to the law that claims the body of a convicted murderer, as it fixes the broad arrow on all its possessions, including convicts, to show for the time being that they were Government property ; the body of a murderer is denied to the relations, the interment must take place where life has been taken from it.

Behind the Prison Chapel at Stafford lies the little cemetery, where the chief actors in some of the most terrible crimes in life are buried side by side, and here, with them, lies Palmer, placed there, in quick lime on his last day.

No loving hands place flowers on the graves, no diligent gardener hoes the weeds ; they are left to seed and seed again, to flower or die as they wish. There, among these graves, is Palmer's, with only the small square stone laid in the brick wall at the head, with his initials and number to mark it, and the tall groundsel that covers its bareness from the world.

Rugeley, after this, found itself so notorious, that a petition was presented to the Premier, Lord Palmerston, praying that the name of the town should be changed.

Whereupon the Premier wittily suggested that the town should be called after himself. Even to-day many articles that belonged to Palmer are treasured possessions of people living in this district.

Palmer's racing stables were situated up the Newport Road near " Dean's Hill."

His jockey, who rode his horse " Rip-Van-Winkle," is still living at the advanced age of 103. He also remembers one of Palmer's victims, who was despatched by the administration of strychnine.

This ends the pages of rogues.

ST. THOMAS' PRIORY.

Ora, Ora, pro nobis.

Situated by the side of the sluggish, shallow River Sowe, about two miles below Stafford, is incorporated in and about the farm and buildings the remains of the priory of black canons founded in 1174, by Bishop Peche, and dedicated by him to St. Thomas of Canterbury. He was associated in this foundation by a citizen of Stafford, who died three years before the edifice was completed.

The Bishop retired to this priory shortly before his own death, in order, possibly, to prepare himself in that holy place for the after life, and no doubt, the mists of bluebells, the placid water, the sight of the distant Milford Hills, must have drawn him to that earthly paradise, as that ecclesiastical atmosphere must have been to his mediæval mind.

On his death, he was buried according to his instructions in front of the high altar, and masses were said daily in that dim sanctuary for the repose of the soul of its priestly founder.

It is not stated where poor Gerap was buried, who probably found most of the money for this colony of monks, and whether any prayers were mumbled for the repose of his soul.

Giles de Erdington obtained the admittance of a Canon into the Priory of St. Thomas' upon his presentation, and that of his heirs to say mass for his family, etc. His name was also to be mentioned in their offices and entered in their Obit List, and his anniversary commemorated.

One hundred years later the great supporter of Simon de Montford, Robert de Ferrers of Tutbury, Earl of Derby, was laid to rest by the side of the Bishop, by his own wish. The Earl presented the Priory with a hospital for the sick. One wonders if a black calf was born in Chartley Park that year. The legend was that the birth of a black calf to one of the herd of wild white British cattle prophesied a death in the family of Ferrers. King Edward II., in his preparations for war against the Scots, became suddenly interested enough in St. Thomas' Priory to require that that institution send supplies to the Royal Army operating in the North against the Scots.

The mandate was issued from York. This was of course some years after the Battle of Bannockburn, where the Scots gained so much English territory, and Edward II. had undertaken that year to recover Berwick-on-Tweed.

In 1326 the little Priory of St. Thomas' had a noble church, with four bells and a clock, and hangings of beautiful material.

They, among other foundations, possessed salt pans in Cheshire, salt being about the only thing these Mediæval monks could not produce in their immediate surroundings, but was also a most important need, as salt was so necessary in the salting down of meat for the winter.

It was during these mediæval times that the curious story of a damsel being pursued, and murdered, in the Priory precincts, causing the Priory to be for ever haunted, must have happened.

All that is known in these pages is the old legend, mentioned before, and at that it must be left in the folds of mystery.

In the course of time came along the suppression of the monasteries and the overthrow of Papal power in this country, by that powerful monarch Henry VIII., whose Minister Cromwell undertoook to pull down the nests. And so the monasteries were gradually suppressed, their contents sold, and the lands granted to the biggest wire-pullers of the times.

The great abbey of Burton, whose Abbots for years had successfully solved unemployment troubles, and first brewed famous Burton Ales, was among them.

Among these larger foundations, which included also Croxden Abbey, the great Cistercian abbey with its farms and infirmary for the poor, passed St. Thomas' Priory ; its monks driven away ; and the goods auctioned to the expectant bargain hunters in Stafford.

Lead made £40 at the sale and the four bells £54. Silver plate was sold weighing 28½oz. (some had already been pledged). The lead was from the roofs and was melted down into " plokes " and " sows," weighed, and marked with the King's marks.

Many abbeys had the lead stripped off the roofs for the King's use, and he had the bells melted down into cannon. The remaining buildings and land of St. Thomas' Priory was granted to Doctor

Note.—There is a curious manorial custom in Warwickshire known as the Collection of Wroth Silver. For the non-payment of these fees a fine is liable of 20s. for every penny or the forfeiture of a white bull with red nose and ears.

The white bull would belong to the ancient wild British cattle such as the Chartley herd, and this clause was probably included by the Lord of the Manor in lieu of the fine as being difficult to obtain and consequently the money would be paid.

Note.—The light of the Catholic Faith first kindled by the monks of Baswich, and continued by the successive chaplains to the Astons, is still kept aglow by the Catholic mission at Great Haywood.

Rowland Lee, Bishop of Lichfied and Coventry, as the See then was, in the year 1539.

At the time of the dissolution its revenues were estimated roughly at £198 per annum. From the Bishop the Priory descended to the Fowler family, who lived on at St. Thomas' Hall, as it was now called, for several centuries. One of the first Fowlers to occupy St. Thomas' was Brian Fowler, who, with his wife Jehan (Hanmer) was buried in the chancel of Baswich Church near by.

Unfortunately this tomb, which was without effigies, was cut into two to make a stairway up to a househould pew.

There is a memorial tablet in the chancel at Berkswich Church recording the names of the Fowler family interred in the church, Fitter's name also included thereon. The inscription also makes allusion to the pronunciation in old English of "jine and joine." A similar reference occurs in Rhoda Broughton's book, a Staffordshire work, entitled "It Cometh Up As a Flower."

In the reign of Charles II., when the Popish agitation was so great, Stephen Dugdale, who knew St. Thomas' very well, laid information while incarcerated in Stafford Gaol, of treason at St. Thomas' Hall. The report stated that Lord Aston, of Tixall, had sent a message over to St. Thomas' to Fr. Fitter, the chaplain, by a woman named Elizabeth Elde. Lord Aston in his letter wished to arrange a secret rendezvous with the priest in a certain field called Brancote, near the river side. The report further stated that after this secret meeting, considered to be of too great importance to be held in the house, where the walls may have ears, the priest went back to the house and told the master's daughter, Miss Fowler, what had passed between him and Lord Aston. Miss Fowler is then reported to have repeated the information to the Elizabeth Elde, who was a trusted agent of Lord Aston, and who had arranged the last meeting. This Elde was purported to come at once to Stafford Gaol and relate the whole to Dugdale. Dugdale then lays his information, that after the treasonable business at Tixall, related earlier in this work, when Dugdale left the house and Lord Aston was so alarmed at Dugdale leaving, with such dangerous knowledge in his possession, that he told the priest Fitter at the subsequent meeting in Brancote field. He went on to say that Lord Aston wept over Fitter, who told him that he wished that he had despatched Dugdale before he had left Tixall.

Later at a trial of two servants of Tixall household, a witness, Sir W. Bagot, J.P., swore that Aston disowned his servant, Dugdale, with the words, "He is no servant of mine."

Dugdale was very unlike a former servant of the Aston's for the quality of loyalty, whose tomb is still to be seen in Tixall churchyard.

The property later passed from the Fowlers to the Spencers, before being divided up between the families of Fowler, Falconberry, and Fitzgerald ; and lastly, in 1765, to the ancestors of Earl Talbot, passing into the Shrewsbury Estates, of which it is still a part. Following its dismantling as a residence, it became a cotton mill.

These cotton printers, who only survived at St. Thomas' for a few years, employed a lot of children, as was the custom of the period, and who were, on each Sunday, instructed by their masters in religious matters. A room was hired in the town and those who undertook the task of instructing these children in the Holy Scriptures not only admitted the little cotton workers, but all children of the poor people of the town, thus carrying on the good work instituted by Robert Raikes at Gloucester.

A few years later saw the abandonment of the cotton concern, and the building became a corn mill until the present time, when the grinding was done away with, and the whole has now become a farm.

To visit this place is now a puzzle, owing to the alterations occasioned by the various uses to which this old habitation has been put since its first inception as a priory of St. Augustine.

The building of the old monks are so mixed up with more recent erections that discernment is difficult. A state of decay covers the whole with a placid mould of neglect. The site of the priory church is but the vacant field of a bare orchard, with but a spindly tree or so to remind the visitor of its fruitful use, while the church is only discernible by the wall and buttresses of the north transcept, with its aumbry, and even the stones of this are falling into oblivion.

Inscription on an Ancient Tomb in Tixall Churchyard.

Heare Lieth Richard Biddulph that was borne in Tixall in the yeare of ovr Lord 1546 and died on thee 15 of Iune
The 82 yeare of his age : He served foure of th Astons : Sr Ed. Aston, Sr M. A. Aston, Sr Ed. Aston and Walter Lord Aston : He was faythfull and diligent in his service
He was loving to his friends : and a iust man towards al.
He was beloved of his masters and having spent his
Whole time in there service : Walter Lord Aston
Payes this acknowledgment to his memorie 1627.

This tomb was restored by the later owners of Tixall, the Cliffords. The female family name Barbara, has descended through both the Astons and Cliffords down to the present day.

EXCAVATIONS.

" The sacred tapers lights are gone,
Grey moss has clad the altar stone,
The holy image is overthrown,
The bell has ceased to toll,
The long ribb'd aisles are burst and shrunk,
The holy shrines to ruin sunk,
Departed is the pious monk,
God's blessing on his soul."　　*Rediveva.*
　　　　Sanctus. Sanctus. Sanctus.

I was invited to join a small body of energetic excavators,

about to make a minute examination of the old ruins of St. Thomas' Priory.

So, accordingly, we assembled on the day appointed with a collection of implements and suitable clothes and soon made our way to " Sentimus," as it is generally pronounced locally. On arrival we immediately got to business, and someone produced a tracing from an old plan of the farm house and buildings, giving also the sites and remaining portions of the monastic foundations that interwind with the rest of the structure so closely as to form a perfect puzzle.

This plan was drawn some fifty years ago by a Mr. Lynam, who was a great archæologist, and preserved among the transactions of the North Staffordshire Field Club in the Salt Library, from where this tracing was taken.

From this plan we were able to make out which formed part of the conventual building, the sites of the cloisters and church. Of the latter only the north transept remains above ground in what constitutes the remains of an old orchard.

We noted, by careful search, here and there in parts of the old priory, first the old tiled floor in the cellar, just as they left it, and with tiles similar to those found about Croxden Abbey. In this cellar is supposed to be a blocked-up entrance to a secret passage leading somewhere or other, but that is all that is known about it.

In the north transept we found an aumbry, where the holy vessels were stored.

In the conventual buildings are the remains of four small carved figures, a small lancet window, and what was possibly a leper's hole.

Our great discovery was on the outer wall of these buildings, on the south side of the buildings near the river. Here, on the huge scarred buttresses that still support this outer wall, too stout, evidently, for the old spoilators to pull down and cart away, are the marks where the bowmen sharpened their arrows and swords during their exercises on holy day, as laid down by a statute of King John, to keep the young men of England " fit." We were very pleased with our first discovery of note, for these arrow marks are rare in Stafford. The reader will note that earlier pages mention the old Mount of Stafford, whose walls were also indented with these marks, and point out that the other nearest local marks of that character are on the Parish Church of Penkridge.

600 years and more ago, on Sunday mornings, between Mass, which was at 11-30 a.m., and Vespers at 2-30 p.m., the youths and men, clad in their Lincoln green, leather belted, with soft brown top-boots and feathered bonnets, would stand by those buttresses and sharpen their steel-tipped arrows in those grooves, and then drew their long bows and aim at targets 150 yards away. What a link these old grooves form with the past, and, near them, I saw the fading mint growing in the garden, and looked to see if it was the same variety of monkish mint found recently at Croxden Abbey, but it wasn't.

The mint growing at Croxden Abbey is very sweet smelling,

and is found growing in large clumps in the precincts of the old Abbey ruins. These masses of luxuriant herb flourish, growing on year after year, multiplying as one can see to this day, increasing in size and sturdiness to combat the grass and weeds, forcing its natural enemies back, gradually gaining mastery over the surrounding herbage, while over all it wafts its sweet smell like an incense, when the wind blows, as if to soften and soothe. There are two reasons that may substantiate its authenticity as being of monkish origin. Firstly, it differs in character from any of the present species of mint that is found either growing wild or in gardens, its leaves being very dark when fully grown and almost circular in shape with much longer stems. Most mints deteriorate if not divided, but these plants occupy the same spot year after year. A second reason is that mint was held sacred to the Virgin Mary in pre-Reformation days, and it is quite conceivable that the monks would plant some of these roots in some special part of their domain, and it would remain there to thrive long after they had ceased to tend it, when most of them had been driven away from the Abbey at its dissolution in the reign of Henry VIII.

The Royal Commissioners, the nobles, etc., who were eager for the gold and land of the abbey and the lead of its roofs, in their greedy haste would not notice these small plants, so that they would escape destruction.

We have deviated, in our keeness, from our business of excavations and hasten round into the old orchard which is to be the scene of our main exploits. As stated, hitherto, the sole remains of the Church were the North Transept, and on Mr. Lynam's plan the foundations of the walls of the Church are indicated by a succession of dotted lines. We decided, first of all, to verify these dotted lines, and, pulling off our coats, paced out the various distances, using the wall of the North Transept as our starting point. Our keenness and excitement knew no bounds ; I knew that several nobles had been buried before the high altar of this Church and how, sometimes, before the monks were dispossessed, they having wind of coming events, would bury much of their plate and wealth about the Priory, and visions rose to my mind of turning up chalices of gold on the ends of our spades and heaving out from under those great slabs, rusted chests, swathed in tree roots and revealing illuminated missals and holy relics falling about in front of my eyes.

So we dug away, and the first check we received was when we found that Mr. Lynam's measurements did not agree with ours, and our most notable discovery was a line of foundation, of a brick wall, not more than 100 years old, a piece of tile, and a very modern-looking oyster shell.

We wondered if our learned predecessor had judged the founda-

Note.—Archangelica, or white dead nettle (Lamium Album). The officinalis was introduced into Scotland by Mary Queen of Scots who used it to prepare a certain liqueur and also for a certain candy, and now grows wild in many parts.

tion by a very marked line of very poor grass running along over the brick foundations. Archæologists often determine, and rightly too, the existence of old foundations by the very poor appearance of the vegetation growing above it.

A silver chalise was actually dug up some years ago on the site of the burial ground of St. Leonard's Hospital (a hospital for lepers, which then included persons with any skin disease).

Nil desperendum being out motto, we decided to dig down immediately by the aumbry in the wall of the transept seeing what foundation the wall boasted and to find out where the line of wall ran from it. We carefully lifted off the covering sods and picked and shovelled immense quantities of earth and a few pieces of sandstone out of a rapidly-widening cavity.

Between two and three feet down we found the transept did possess various knobbly projections that evidently passed for a foundation. Then our spades struck something very hard and firm, and by the dint of much puffing and blowing, revealed what looked like part of the old pavement of the Church Priory.

There was a general pause in our labour . . . .

FINIS.

Fragments—just fragments ; broken pieces of a puzzle, put together with but an error here and there, as occurs in all things historical.

APPENDIX.

A letter from Charles I. written at Stafford in the year 1642 to Prince Rupert :

CHARLES R.

Our will and pleasure is that you give orders immediately to 8 troops of Horse and 5 troops of Dragooners, Under the command of some such person Whom you shall think fitt for this service, to march tomorrow towards Nantwich, and to quarter upon Tuesday night in some convenient place near unto Nantwich, and then to remayne until you shall receive further directions either from Us, or from our right trusty and well-beloved the Lord Strange, or in his absence from our Commissioners of Army for our County of Cheshire, wch directions they are punctually to obey, and for your so doing this shall be sufficient warrant.

Given att our Court att Stafford this 18th of September, 1642.

To our dear Nephew Prince Rupert, Generall of our Horse.

Letter to the High Sheriff of Staffordshire, Sir Edward Mosley, of Rolleston :

CHARLES R.

Our will and pleasure is, and we doe hereby command and authorise you to raise sufficient forces of horse and foote, to bee paid by the county, and to putt the same into the Castle of Tutbury, for the defence and securetie of the same against all leavies, of the rebels, and other illaffected persons in that or the neighbouring counties. And we hereby require you to use your utmost industry with our well affected subjects in that our countie, to persuade them to contribute horse, armies, ammunition, plate, or money, to us for our assistance and defence.

And we doe hereby authorise you, by yourselfe, or such fitt persons as you shall appoynt on that behalf to receive the same.

And you are to return to Us a list of their names and contributions that we may make them satisfaction when God shall enable us, and remember it upon all occasions to their advantage.

And we require and authorise you to convene all the gentlemen, clergie, freeholders, and other well affected subjects of our county to the purpose afforesaid.

And for soe doing this shall bee your sufficient warrant.

Given att our Courte of Reddeinge on the 26th November, 1642.

www.ingramcontent.com/pod-product-compliance
Lightning Source LLC
Chambersburg PA
CBHW051843040426
42447CB00006B/676